W9-AAV-838

Accumulated Appreciation

A CAREER GUIDE FOR ACCOUNTING MAJORS

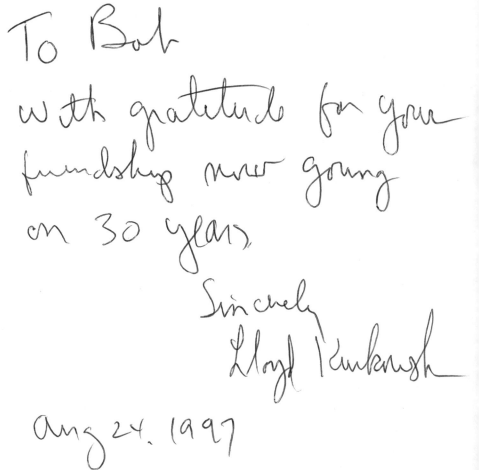

To Bob

with gratitude for your
friendship never going
on 30 years.

Sincerely
Lloyd Kunkrush

Aug 24. 1997

Accumulated Appreciation

A Career Guide for Accounting Majors

Lloyd Kurkowski

Sulzburger & Graham Publishing, Ltd.
New York

Wheaties, Spuds MacKenzie, "Know when to say when," Budweiser, Gillete, "Look sharp—Be sharp", Cadillac, Bombay, Hyatt Hotels, Gallup Poll, and Red Heart Dog Food are registered trademarks.

Sulzburger & Graham Publishing, Ltd.
505 Eighth Avenue New York, NY 10018
© 1997 by Lloyd Kurkowski
All rights reserved. Published 1997
Printed in the United States of America

ISBN 1-57613-000-5

To Joyce,
who brought me the real meaning of love—as my wife,
companion, and mother of John and Ann.

Contents

Part III. *Forty Years in the Financial World—Reflections and Experiences*

Acknowledgments

As a first time author, I was fortunate to have great business professionals as my devil's advocates. Their help was enormous—Frank Hianik, Bill O'Meara, and Jerry Farr who worked with me at Price Waterhouse, John Morrell & Company, and Jane Dickson who worked with me at John Morrell & Company and my consulting practices. Lastly, to my son, John, and daughter, Ann, whose viewpoints as young business professionals were invaluable in shaping this book for my intended audience of young accountants and accounting students.

Introduction

I landed on planet Earth on May 27, 1923, in LaSalle, Illinois, the first born of John and Marie Kurkowski. The cliche about choosing parents wisely certainly applied to me—they had adequate financial means, but were millionaires if you put a dollar amount on love, family values, and togetherness. I was doubly lucky in another respect—starting life in 1923 was a ringside seat to view the roaring twenties, the 1929 stock market crash and the great depression, World War II, the coming of computers and the jet age, the rise and fall of Communism, and many technologies that produced television, transistors, medical achievements, etc., that improved one's quality of life and extended their life span by many years. These milestones will surely be cited when historians and sociologists write about the incredible twentieth century. Hidden among these remarkable developments (and probably not to be mentioned by writers) is the emergence of the accounting profession and its silent role as a contributor and a member of the support groups that played significant roles in mankind's progress in this century. As a career financial professional, I spent forty years in the financial world and clearly saw just how important modern day accounting is to any business or organization, past, present, and probably to a greater extent, future.

I was lucky to choose accounting as my life's occupation. During my childhood, I had a number of ambitions and career ideas—sports, music, and medicine to name a few. But after serving three years as a navigator in the Army Air Force, I returned to college in 1946 and settled on a new goal—the world of business, with marketing as my specialty. During my postwar study at the University of Illinois, I ran into class schedule difficulties one semester and was literally forced to take an accounting course to meet semester hour requirements. To my great surprise, I really enjoyed

1

the course and easily earned an A grade. I then switched my major from marketing to accounting, and earned straight A's in all accounting courses, and passed the CPA exam during my last semester in school. After graduation, I started my accounting career with Price Waterhouse and spent forty interesting and satisfying years in various senior positions in the financial world.

Upon reaching my 65th birthday, I retired from business and started the very pleasant retirement years. Family travel, golf and other sports, and volunteer financial advisory work kept me quite busy. However, I felt that I should do something a little more constructive. Quite suddenly it crossed my mind that I could put the experiences of my career to good use by writing a book for college accounting majors, and write it in such a way that would be helpful to a student still in school and those in their first few years on the job.

After a number of stops and starts, and helpful advice and encouragement from my family and former business associates, I finally completed the book. What I hope to accomplish is to leave you better prepared and more knowledgeable about what lies ahead in the financial world—the different accounting and financial positions and what they are really like, and a host of very important accounting related applications that you undoubtedly did not cover in the classroom. This book should help you in your job selection and the things that you must do to ultimately attain the optimum position commensurate with your technical knowledge, capabilities, and your own self-development. Specifically, the book touches on all the essentials to get to the top and the importance of nonaccounting skills such as getting along well with people, effective speaking and writing, the need for ongoing setting of goals as well as personal development and time management, and lastly, the obvious requirement of integrity and professionalism in every job and every assignment.

There are three parts to this book.

Part I. Ladies and Gentlemen Start Your Engines—It's Time for Work

This part covers the extreme importance of your first job and what you must do to avoid the pitfalls of getting started on a job that is not compatible with your talent, potential, and career objectives. It also covers the need for continued self-development, and the work and life habits that you must establish and follow in order to achieve and maintain maximum potential in your business career.

Part II. Important Financial World Observations and Applications

Four years of accounting academia cannot possibly cover all the important accounting and financial applications you are sure to experience sometime during your career. This part includes a number of them which you probably didn't cover very thoroughly in school. It includes strategic planning, taxes, product line profitability, mergers and acquisitions, and a number of other significant topics.

Part III. Forty Years in the Financial World—Reflections and Experiences

Starting with seven years of CPA experience with Price Waterhouse, I proceeded throughout my career to hold senior accounting and financial positions with large and small public companies, and large private companies. I was also the president of a growing insurance company, a partner in a successful consulting firm, and served on the board of directors of several companies. These positions are all important in the financial world, and while they all have a number of common threads, they are sufficiently unique so that each position gives a different look and/or insight for the business involved. This part is written to give the reader a snapshot and the flavor of all these positions using experiences and practical examples. I believe this section will help you determine exactly what position in the financial world appears to be best for you.

****

I wrote this book as a sort of legacy to society. It is a thank-you for the good fortunes and good life that I've enjoyed. My fondest hope is that every reader will benefit, in some way. That alone will make my time and effort worthwhile.

Part I.

Ladies and Gentlemen Start Your Engines–
It's Time for Work

Chapter 1

Your First Job—A Critical Decision

If I had been asked the question "Did you choose the best career?" my answer ten years ago, today, and ten years from now would be the same. "I'm not sure, but I can say that overall I enjoyed my career very much; it afforded me intellectual challenge, interesting business achievements, great camaraderie, and an income level that has enabled my family to enjoy a first-class lifestyle." Looking back, my career ambitions changed a number of times in my life. In grammar school I was a football junkie, and of course, I was going to the University of Notre Dame to play football and then become a football coach. In high school I became enamored with jazz piano and my next ambition was to become the pianist for the great Glen Miller band. After three years in the U.S. Army Air Force, I returned to civilian life all fired up about getting into a noble profession like medicine, education, or our country's diplomatic corps. As I neared graduation from the University of Illinois in late 1947, I decided on a new career objective—marketing combined with accounting. I was thoroughly convinced that I had the needed outgoing personality for selling, and combined with my accounting skills, I could project myself as a future senior marketing executive with IBM. Sounds great, but it never got off the ground. Sort of like the Broadway musical *A Funny Thing Happened on the Way to the Forum.* In my case, "the funny thing" about my becoming an IBM marketing executive made a sharp turn, when after talking to my very good friend and accounting professor C.A. Moyer, I took the CPA exam at his suggestion, passed it all, and then accepted employment with Price Waterhouse, which at the time was either number one or two among the Big Six. This was the kickoff that started the inertia to carry me through a forty- year career in the financial community. Although I was never the sales and marketing executive I had planned to be, I found that I used my outgoing skills a great deal throughout my career as a financial officer. The fact that I had a successful and enjoyable business career was certainly due in part to pure luck. What I hope to impress upon you is the importance of being better prepared than I was when you start looking for your first real job.

Okay, here we are in your senior year of college and you are nearing graduation. What is your game plan? If you are a top student you would make a wise decision if you include a master's degree in your plan. If you have investment banking in your bonnet, it is an absolute must to have postgraduate work to have some chance for employment in this coveted field of finance. As to timing, I personally believe it is better to first take a job for a year or two and get a feel for the financial world before starting your work on a master's degree. If your finances allow it, getting your degree as a full-time student is probably the best way to go about it. However, getting it as a part-time student at night school can be just as good if you have the time and endurance.

But for most college accounting majors, the initial objective as graduation nears is the selection of a first job. It can be one of the most critical decisions in a person's life, and yet so frequently the decision is made too quickly and without adequate thought or preparation. The result can be a very unhappy person who never achieves his/her optimum potential, and because of financial responsibilities either becomes frustrated and trapped in a miserable job for his/her entire career or constantly moves from job to job never finding job satisfaction or the opportunity to utilize skills and education.

There are a number of major mistakes a graduate can make in the job selection process. Here is my laundry list of the major mistakes I've seen graduates make:

1) They attach too much importance to the starting salary and not enough to the many important nonsalary benefits and future opportunities.

2) They accept positions that are obviously not up to their intellectual capabilities and offer little chance for job challenge and growth.

3) They don't do enough homework on the prospective employer. Is it a winner? Is the company in good financial condition? Is it growing? Does it have a good image in the financial and civic communities?

4) They don't find out enough about what the future opportunities are—promotions, salary increases, training and scholastic programs, perks, etc.
5) They fail to inquire about the possibility of a transfer to another division or subsidiary. (Students with irrevocable hometown roots should scratch a prospective employer in which a transfer to another city might be expected at some stage of employment. As an example, for years IBM was considered the acronym for "I've Been Moved.")
6) They simply do not prepare adequately for their job interviews.

These suggestions are pretty much standard and would be appropriate to consider by all college graduates in the job hunting process.

The graduating accounting major has five basic job categories they can explore. They are:

1) Public accounting with a big firm
2) Public accounting with a small firm
3) Private accounting with a big firm
4) Private accounting with a small firm
5) Taxation via the IRS

Let's talk first about public accounting with the Big Six. If you look at the who's who of chief executive officers (CEOs), chief financial officers (CFOs), treasurers, and controllers, you will find that the lion's share of them had experience with the Big Six. I had seven years with Price Waterhouse and in forty years in the financial community, I dealt with all of the other major CPA firms—they are all tops, and it is a wonderful way to get a practical "Ph.D." in accounting. The job demands are not for the fainthearted. The competition is tough, the work is very challenging, and the hours are sometimes long and arduous. But it is a marvelous opportunity to get experience and insight into many different industries and companies that are assigned to you via your annual client audit schedule. I also enjoyed meeting new and interesting people as I went from one audit client to another. Moreover, the periodic travel was also a pleasant change of pace. All of the Big Six firms have expanded their professional staffs and now have specialists in management consulting, strategic planning, pension and actuarial, executive recruitment, etc. These areas of expertise offer potential employment opportunities for capable staff members who find that pure auditing is not their cup of tea. If after, say, five or six years with a Big Six firm you decide that it is in your best interest to leave the world of the big CPA firms you can be assured that you have the right credentials for a good financial position in the business world.

There are many excellent medium-sized CPA firms who have fairly well-staffed local or regional offices. Some of these firms are just a shade below the Big Six in prestige and opportunities, so if you can't get on with a Big Six firm getting on the staff of a good regional firm would still be a good start for a graduating accounting major who wants to make a career with a CPA firm, or utilize the experience of five or six years as a springboard to a good accounting position in industry.

If you look in the yellow pages of a telephone directory for a medium-sized city, you will find CPA listings by the hundreds. I'm sure there are employment opportunities with many of these small firms and sole practitioners, and it's possible that the initial starting salary could be as good as you find with a Big Six firm. Unfortunately, you will probably find that the business is largely bookkeeping, monthly and quarterly statements, and tax preparation: not much in the way of intellectual challenge, and a certainty for job boredom and a limited career path. If you have an ambitious career plan and are capable and hard working, then avoid this kind of job if you can. Moreover, this kind of employment experience is worth very little on your future personal resume.

Public accounting, big or small, is not for everyone. Each job is a new and sometimes unsettling experience—a new boss (the manager or partner), new surroundings (the client's office), new work associates (the client's staff and your own working associates), new and different accounting problems (the client's unique system) and finally, unpredictable audit crises and long hours of work. However, in the long run the hard work will reward you handsomely as you move to the upper ranks of the CPA firms or to an important position in industry.

Students who prefer a more stable and predictable job environment would do well to avoid the public accounting field and try to get on an accounting staff of a good solid public company. A Fortune 1000 company would be the first choice, because many of these firms have extensive training programs and offer excellent career opportunities. Many smaller public companies also have good training programs and career opportunities. You will have to research the field and target those that fit your objectives.

Later in this book I point out that some private companies operate exactly like public companies, and your job research may lead you to an excellent private company with fine career opportunities. However, beware of a job with a private company that seems to be stagnant and/or reeking with nepotism. Also, if possible, avoid employment with very small private companies because they generally don't offer many worthwhile career opportunities.

For graduates who have an interest in taxes, it is obvious that they should be looking at the Internal Revenue Service (IRS) as a starting point for a career in the field of taxation. Their hours are pretty much nine to five, which affords ample evening time for the ambitious graduate who would like to get a law degree via night school and weekend study. That, coupled with IRS experience and an accounting major, is a beautiful combination. But one thing is certain—you must like taxes or forget it.

Summer employment and summer training programs are practical exposures into certain industries and certain jobs. Those students with that experience have a head start on job hunting because they already have had the opportunity to look over potential jobs and find out what they like and don't like. Moreover, they have experienced what it's like to be an employee and the responsibilities and discipline required to be a good employee. I have always had a lot more respect for college students who divide their summer equally between work and fun. It is a real plus on your resume to have had summer employment.

It is my hope that you will get many good ideas from this book, but if you only get *one*, I think the following can be one of the most significant: "Go to the library and browse through some of the many books on interviews, and then make the appropriate preparations."

Make no bones about it, jobs are won and lost in the interview. For most graduates they will be experiencing their first interview. Think about it, what have you done well the first time you tried it? Even the gifted athlete who swings at a golf ball for the first time either whiffs it or slices it out of bounds. So what makes you think you can walk into a room with a personnel director without painstaking preparation, and win the Mr. Smooth Award?

Here are some highlighted points summarized from good books on interviews that you will want to follow:

1) Know something about the company that is interviewing you
2) Look sharp
3) Be on time
4) Use your own technique to keep nervousness under control

5) The all-important handshake with the interviewer should be firm, but not a death grip, and be accompanied by a smile and good eye contact when you introduce yourself.

6) Be honest and answer the questions as best you can. If you don't know an answer don't be afraid to say "I don't know," and by all means don't answer questions with half-truths, fibs, or statements you think the interviewer wants to hear. The professional interviewer can easily pick these things out and will probably give you a flunking grade on your interview.

It goes without saying that every interview will include at least one of these very important questions:

1) Tell me about yourself
2) Where do you want to be in five years?

These are the two subjects that you should concentrate on, and in preparing for them, I suggest that you have a mock interview with your roommate or a close friend acting out the part of the interviewer. It is good experience and a confidence builder for you, and at the same time, your friend could be a useful devil's advocate.

After the first interview, you'll find that each succeeding interview is a little easier, and you are much more effective. It is obvious then, that you should not interview with your target company until you've had a few interviews with similar firms that are not quite as important to you.

If you have a good academic record, a good listing of life credentials, and have interviewed well, you are virtually assured of getting a pretty good job offer. But because of economic conditions, bad luck, bad timing, or whatever, you may not receive an offer from your campus interviews. Shortly you will be heading home with your diploma and a degree, but without a job. What's your plan? Here are some suggestions.

1) Prepare a resume and take it to the placement office for their critique and suggestions. Leave a copy of your finished resume with the placement office so that they can continue assisting you in your job search.

2) Contact all of the companies who interviewed you and try to find out why you weren't selected. You may learn something about yourself that you were not aware of. Hopefully, it's eas-

ily repairable. If it isn't, you've got to face up to the problem and do something about it.

3) Prepare a specific plan for your job search, i.e., the business category and the companies in that category that interest you, the kind of position you are seeking, the salary range, and any other requirements you may have.

4) Aggressively and quickly contact all those companies in 3) using resumes, phone calls, introductions through friends, etc.

5) As your job search unfolds you should be receiving feed back about your credentials, your academic record, personality, appearance, and communication skills. This may be the signal for you to start a self-development program which will vastly improve your chances of getting a good job. It may require night school, CPA review courses, and other study programs. But what does it matter if it takes another year as long as it helps you in your career program?

Job hunting can be a very tiring and frustrating experience. Nevertheless, you should promise yourself that you'll work at it every day, and not sit around and become a lush on your parents' income. While you struggle to find the job in your career plan, you should definitely try to find some kind of job to pay for your living expenses, and avoid getting into a lazy pattern. There are employment opportunities, no matter the state of our country's economy. I'm sure you can meet the challenge and find an interim job.

Chapter 2

A Quantum Leap—From the Campus to the Workplace

My son graduated from the University of Illinois in 1988, and my daughter is currently in graduate school at Rush St. Luke University. Our attendance at homecoming, parents weekend, football games, and other activities have kept us close to campus life for the past eight years. Oh yes, there have been changes. The University of Illinois is twice as big as it was when I graduated, and there are coed dormitories which were an absolute no-no back then. But a lot of things haven't changed at all—our Friday beer bashes were no different than the Thursday keg parties of today except that we were a little older (postwar GIs) and were better chug-a-luggers (with tongue in cheek we bragged that we were responsible for Anheuser–Busch starting a second shift). We dressed in rags or leftover military garb, except on weekends when we would don our gray flannel suit or navy blazer if we had a big date. Today the guys, at least, are in rags everyday including the weekends. Back then and still today, eight o'clock classes are avoided like the plague, and the morning wake-up is twenty minutes before the first class. Breakfast was either nothing or a greasy doughnut, and cutting classes was standard as it still is. In short, college life overall was and still is a wonderful, challenging, and an unforgettable four-year experience. However, the environment of the workplace is a sharp contrast from the freewheeling pace of campus living. As you start your first job, there are a number of necessary disciplines and work habits that you should start from day one and maintain throughout your business career. Remember, habits are hard to break, so if you start with good habits and keep them, your journey in business will be much easier. Most of the following are old hat, common sense rules of conduct, but I'm including them as part of your job check list.

Be on Time

You surely will not be late your first day of work, but what will your on-time record be for the first full year? It is very easy to start slipping into the habit of five minutes late then ten minutes, etc., especially if a lot of other people are habitually late and are not reprimanded. Don't fall into the trap of following the other guy. The employee who is on time day-in and day-out and who follows the affixed hours for lunch, closing time, etc., is noticed and is quietly adding good points to their personnel file.

Be a Good Soldier

Whether it be the military or a sports training camp, the new kid on the block is bound to get some sort of initiation or hazing. So don't get ticked off if you receive menial work assignments at first. It's a way of paying your dues, and at the same time, the employer wants to look you over before giving you any challenging work. It may be the first time in your life that you are taking orders, and you may not care too much about some of the orders you receive nor agree with them. Nevertheless, you must be the "good soldier" and carry out the orders to the best of your ability. This is a discipline you have to learn and retain as long as you are an employee. Everyone has a boss. Even if you ultimately become the chairman of the board of directors, you still have a boss—namely, the outside directors on the board as well as the corporation's stockholders. You are free from orders and a boss only when you retire.

Be a Good Listener

Until you've learned the territory, concentrate on doing a lot of listening so that you really understand your assignment and the routine of the workplace. One way to rub veteran employees the wrong way is for the new college kid to start expounding right away. Naturally, you will be very eager to put your academic theories to use. However, you may have to curb that enthusiasm and wait for the proper time.

Be Honest

I never dealt with too many people who were out and out liars, but I dealt with many people who were cheaters, told half-truths or little fibs, or who could twist words in such a way as to accomplish a lie. Eventually, these people get caught and when they do they get the reputation that they can't be trusted, a label that is disastrous on an employee's record. It's not easy to be totally honest. Sometimes it might seem perfectly right to bend the rules. Let me give you a couple examples.

Example 1

An auditor is working on inventories and runs into some unexpected problems on obsolescence. The auditor wants to hold the total audit hours to a certain number and knows that the obsolescence problem will cause an overrun. So the auditor looks for a safe harbor and concludes that they can save hours by initialing certain PBC (preferred by client) schedules as having done 100% of the work (vouching or whatever) even though they may only have checked 10 % of the schedule.

Example 2

An employee has an out of town assignment requiring air travel to a subsidiary. This employer does not have a lot of restrictions on travel expense. The employee takes the bus to the airport for $1.00, carries their bag to the hotel room, and skips breakfast the following morning. When the employee makes out the expense report, they record: "cab to airport, $16.00, tip to porter, $2.00, and breakfast, $5.75." These expenses will never be questioned and the employee knows it. The employee's rationalization for doing this is that they spent about $25.00 that night cruising the bars, and felt justified in making up the amount.

Like any habit, once it's started, inertia sets in place and it accelerates and only worsens. I don't have to tell you right from wrong; just start your career with a promise that no matter what the situation, you will be totally honest and ethical in all of your employment activities. In the long run, you will be richer and wiser for it.

Be a Cool Cat

It's very hard to keep your emotional button under control at all times. We all have different fuses, but some have fuses so short that they explode at the slightest provocation. There will be times when you are the fall guy for your boss who bungled an important assignment, or you've worked like a Trojan for months preparing a scholarly report, only to have one of your over-the-hill supervisors shout it down for no reason other than "We've never done it that way!" It's not easy to keep your cool; it takes character and discipline to develop the aplomb for those demanding situations. President Reagan was a perfect example of a man who never got ruffled, shouted out of control, or let an adversary box him in. In your first year or two it is unlikely that you will be directly involved in these kinds of situations, but you may be present when your superiors are. Watch closely, listen attentively, and you'll see how important this skill is, and what it takes to be the "winner."

Be a Jack Armstrong

For many years Jack Armstrong was on the Wheaties cereal box as the "All-American Boy." In the glory days of radio, the nightly Jack Armstrong program was a must for all teenagers. He was the star athlete for mythical Hudson High that won every athletic event on the last play of the game thanks to Jack's last second heroics. Jack was Mr. Perfect. He got eight hours of sleep, ate a Wheaties breakfast, of course, and was in peak physical condition. Those three daily rules of living are terribly important because of the pressure and challenge of your work. If you aren't bright-eyed and bushy-tailed when you start the workday, the fatigue factor will hit you like a ton of bricks before your workday is two-thirds complete. Just make sure to start a daily regimen for your workday that includes the right amount of sleep, exercise, and sensible eating, and you will be able to perform well for the full day.

Be a Telephone Nonuser

With the proliferation of the 1-800 number and direct dialing, it can be very tempting for office workers to do their shopping, stock investments, and endless socializing on the company telephones. Do yourself a favor, starting with your first day of employment: vow that on company time you will make personal phone calls only when they are absolutely necessary (calling your spouse to tell them you will be on a later train, etc.). Moreover, do whatever you have to do to eliminate or hold to a minimum, incoming phone calls from investment brokers, telemarketing salesmen, and friends. The incoming calls always seem to come at the worst time, and it really is an irritant to management when meetings are interrupted by outside calls. If you become smitten with telephonitis, you will eventually get the reputation that you're always on the phone, and I promise you, that label will not generate any gold stars in your personnel file.

Be like Spuds MacKenzie

In one of the Budweiser Beer commercials three women sing a little ditty to the Budweiser dog Spuds MacKenzie, heaping great praise on Spuds because he "knows when to say when." If you imbibe in alcoholic beverages pay heed to these suggestions, because good management of your alcohol intake is an absolute must for a successful career.

1) Know how much alcohol you can handle safely.
2) The night before a workday, don't have more than two drinks before dinner and don't drink after dinner.
3) Don't have a drink at lunch as part of your usual lifestyle. On special occasions such as celebrating a successful audit, one drink is not out of order.
4) If you go astray and get drunk the night before a workday, don't show up for work reeking of booze. You are better off to call in sick and vow not to let it happen again.
5) If you find that you are frequently reporting for work in various degrees of a hangover, then you should seek professional help.

What you drink on your weekends is of course your own business, but "knowing when to say when" is a good rule for every day of the year.

Be a Nonuser of Tobacco and Drugs

This is so obvious that I won't insult your intelligence with commenting—by now you certainly know better.

Be a Good Worker

While the foregoing do's and don'ts are all relatively important in your total behavior pattern while on the job, perhaps the most significant bit of advice I can give you is: "be a good worker."

In simple summary this means that you know your assignments and job responsibilities and you carry them out as a professional, completing them correctly, on time, and without any fanfare. It means that you conduct yourself with loyalty to the company at all times, and with consideration and cooperation in all of your associations with other employees. It also means that you never bad mouth either the company or your fellow employees. If there are problems with the company or fellow employees don't let it gnaw you to pieces. Talk it over with your supervisor and see if the matter can be resolved, because you can't be an effective worker if you are not a happy worker.

One of the things that has always amazed me is the different performance levels from employees who are intellectually the same—one will complete an assignment beautifully with no loose ends, and the other will drag their feet and never really complete the assignment at all. The doers seem to stand out. They have initiative, drive, and are always full of hustle. They thrive on being busy, giving rise to the expression, "if you want something done, give it to a busy person." The non-doers are usually lazy, they spend far too much time gossiping and reading *The Wall Street Journal* and other publications. When they settle down to work, they invariably go at it incorrectly, take forever to do it, and never finish the assignment in tip-top condition. You know the final outcome don't you? In time the non-doers are reading the want ads and talking to personnel placement organizations, while the doers have moved up the ladder in their respective organizations.

I want to emphasize that being a good worker does not mean being a workaholic. As professionals, it is inevitable that you will have deadlines and demands that require overtime from time to time but not as a continuing occurrence. I want to talk a little about the employee who constantly stays late at the office or is forever taking work home and often subtly lets you know how late they stayed or how long they were working on company matters. I have always been wary of these "workaholics," and have found them to be less than top quality employees. There are all kinds of workaholics—both real and fake. My advice is to be wary of the "workaholics" who persistently let you know how hard they work and all the long hours they put in.

****

The common sense work habits that I have suggested you adopt, starting with you first day of employment, will go a long way toward maximizing your career potential. They are relatively simple, and undoubtedly you've heard these work rules from other sources in different ways many times. But I want to reiterate—they work and will pay handsome dividends if you have the discipline to stick by them.

Chapter 3

Look Sharp and Be Sharp

Our country's colleges and universities turn out thousands of capable accounting majors each year, many of whom are in the upper ten percent of their class, sport a high grade point average, and have a collection of scholastic honors. All of you in this select group have the proven brainpower and intellectual achievements to make it to the top—some will, but a surprising number will not. Why? Because they didn't develop all of the nonacademic skills necessary. That is what this chapter is all about. It's simple, grassroots common sense about communication skills, appearance, and behavior, most of which you've heard time and again from your mother, father, grandparents, aunts, uncles, big brother, sister, and friends next door. But most teenagers are not good listeners (especially when their parents are talking), and those pearls of wisdom usually go in one ear and out the other. Mark Twain really summed it up beautifully in his famous joke about the "young man who upon reaching his twenty-first birthday was amazed at how smart his father had become in the last two years."

Have you ever attended an annual stockholders' meeting of a major corporation? If you haven't, I'll describe a more typical one because it's a good example of charm at work. They are usually held in a large conference room in a plush hotel. The room will be nicely decorated; there will be refreshments and product displays in the back of the room, and corporate staff personnel will be on hand to mingle with the stockholders, socialize, and explain the products. At the appointed time, the meeting will be called to order, and the company's chairman, CEO, and other senior officers will walk onto center stage. The meeting will be under way. What you will see is four or five executives who are dressed perfectly in fine business attire, and they will be well groomed. As the meeting progresses, they will make the usual presentations, and you'll find most of them to be articulate and very good speakers. When it comes time for the stockholders to ask questions, the executives will handle them with finesse, readiness, and clarity. When the meeting is over (about an hour), the stockholders usually leave with the feeling that their investment is in good hands. They have just witnessed a smooth and winning performance by a group of seasoned business executives who demonstrated the skills and knowhow that comes with years of extra training, practice, and development.

There is one further observation I would like to make about the people who make it to the top. It seems that the majority are good-looking with fine physical dimensions. Moral of the story: it doesn't hurt to be good-looking, but if you're not, you can still have a winning appearance if you take care of yourself and follow a charm school program. The first order of business has to be the procurement of an appropriate wardrobe for your first job. If you are starting with a Big Six CPA firm or a major corporation, you should start building a wardrobe so that ultimately you can wear a different suit or outfit each day of the work week. (And for God's sake, take your father and mother along when you go shopping. They will know what styles are in good taste and what the fashion extremes are that should be excluded from a business wardrobe. After all, most of you have been locked into jeans and sweat shirts for four years of college, and probably half of the boys can't even tie a windsor knot!) Rounding out the rest of the wardrobe with matching shirts, blouses, and accessories such as ties and jewelry is very important, as is several pairs of good shoes that should be polished at all times. I know that this may sound like a Sergeant Major barking out instructions for a white glove military inspection. The fact is that in the real business world, the people who consistently look neat and well-groomed have a big advantage over the employees who wear unattractive clothing and shoes that simply are not in style or in good taste.

Your boss's perception of your work is terribly influenced by how you look. Besides your wardrobe, it is important that you wear your hair in keeping with current style. I don't think the men will win points by such hair extremes as a shaved head or hair hanging below the shoulders. I'm not up to speed on women's hairdos, but most women seem to have hairstyles in good taste already.

It is obviously not too difficult or time consuming to get a nice wardrobe and at least look the part of a business professional. What starts to separate the men from the boys and the women from the girls is what happens when you open your mouth and start to speak. Just how good are you in spontaneous conversation, whether one-on-one or with a group? Can you be comfortable and confident in conversations with new acquaintances? Can you handle public speaking?

Let me tell you my experiences on the matter of public speaking. My first introduction to speaking came in a debating class in my freshmen year of college. I rather liked it, and with my classmate George Pletch (who later became a senior partner at a prestigious Chicago law firm) we were the debating "champs" that year. In the military I had to make introductory speeches to aviation cadets from time to time, and at Price Waterhouse I made a few short speeches to small dinner groups. I was therefore not a totally inexperienced speaker when the CEO of John Morrell & Company asked me to make an address at the company's management staff meeting. My topic was to describe the accounting changes planned for the ensuing fiscal year. I outlined my speech on index cards and had no fears or nervousness about making the speech. (Perhaps that should have been a warning.) After I was introduced, I sailed right into my presentation and was proceeding nicely when the CEO got up and came over to adjust the microphone. When I resumed speaking I started hearing mike-echoes, and I started fighting it. In a matter of seconds I was overwhelmed with mike fright. While I might not remember what I ate for dinner last night, I still remember the terror of that experience with the mike thirty years ago as if it was yesterday. My mouth and lips dried-up like the desert, and my vocal chords were paralyzed. I could barely open my mouth, and when I did, not a word would come out. The best way I can describe the feeling is that it is similar to what happens when your dentist gives you an injection of novocaine before drilling, except that this same feeling extended to my whole body. In those few seconds, I prayed, clenched my fist, and made eye contact with a good friend in the front row. That's what did it. I started giving my speech directly to him, and in a minute or two I had fully regained my composure and finished the speech satisfactorily.

Afterwards, I vowed I would not let that happen again. I would do whatever it took to become a good speaker. I bought books on speaking, and I practiced at home by giving after-dinner talks to my family. This was helpful, but the real turnaround came when I accidentally learned of the Toastmasters' Club. This is a wonderful worldwide organization with members from all walks of life and one common goal—to improve their public speaking skills. You can join for a modest amount (about twenty-five dollars), and the group meets about every two or three weeks, usually around 6:00 PM for dinner at a private dining room. You will make a short speech of some sort at practically every meeting and occasionally a longer speech. You participate and critique all the speeches made during the meeting, and while it is also a lot of fun, you will find that you gradually conquer your speaking flaws and show marked improvement as a speaker. In my case this was certainly true. I became chairman of the American Meat Institute Accounting Committee, and in that role I conducted two- and three-day seminars for audiences of several hundred people. I got to the point that I looked forward to these events because I liked the challenge. Even though I now had the confidence, you can rest assured that I never made a speech without that adrenaline rushing through me five minutes before it was showtime.

I don't believe good oral communication skills are God-given; it is a skill that has to be developed. It's unlikely that the typical graduating college senior has a lot of speaking experience, and it is almost certain that you will not be called on to make major public speeches in your first few years of employment. However, more than likely you will be making mini speeches day-in and day-out to your bosses and associates. Some might be very extemporaneous. For example, the CEO may ask the controller about a troublesome problem with vendor payments, and it ends up that you are called upon to explain how the mess happened in the accounts payable department. You may not know it, but you are now on center stage. If you articulate well, it can really help your career development.

I can't emphasize the importance of developing your speaking skills enough, so don't overlook any opportunity you may have to acquire experience, i.e., be a reader at Sunday service in your church or join civic organizations and young groups such as the Boy Scouts or Girl Scouts that require numerous speaking requirements. The best training ground I found was the Toastmasters' organization. However, their program extends over a long period and may not be the best time schedule for you. In which case, a crash, night school speaking course at a college or university might work out better.

Being able to write effectively is also important and necessary in the development of a successful business executive. Review your grades in Rhetoric, English, and any writing courses you took. If they do not average out to at least a B it would surely indicate that you are weak in this skill and need further study, practice, and experience. The one thing you don't want to do is submit a written report to your boss replete with misspelled words and grammatical errors. It obviously creates a very negative impression about the total person. There is no better example than Vice President Dan

Quayle's disastrous incident when he mistakenly told a grammar school student that potato should be spelled "potatoe."

I would really be remiss if I did not include this observation on a very important but frequently overlooked aspect of a charm school degree—personal hygiene. I would like to have ten dollars for each time I sat next to people in meetings who were reeking with body odor, bad breath, or had dirty fingernails. There really isn't any excuse for this, and it therefore gives the bad impression that if the person is careless about personal hygiene, he or she must be even more careless about their work. Don't take chances. Make sure you start the day with a shower, fresh clothing, deodorant, and mouth wash. For a little insurance, it is not a bad idea to carry a breath spray for mid-morning and mid-afternoon freshening up.

Lastly, but surely one of your most important assets or liabilities, is how well you get along with people. For some, trying to be nice is harder for them than trying to pick up mercury—it's impossible. For others it's easy and natural. Where do you stand on a scale of one to ten? If you honestly analyze yourself and have a pretty good grade, then be especially thankful to your parents who shaped your sense of values, good manners, and good morals. If your self examination shows a number of weaknesses— a hot temper, laziness, a tendency to be bigoted, and other behavioral no-no's—then it is apparent that you've got some serious problems that need to be corrected. Spend a few hours some evening at your local library and browse through Dale Carnegie's *How to Win Friends and Influence People*—over fifteen million copies have been sold. That should be convincing evidence of the book's integrity and readership value. Of course, you will find a number of other equally good books that also can be very helpful in your development of a likeable and winning personality. But remember to be patient, because it takes a lot of time and effort to change ingrained behavioral traits.

In the musical classic *My Fair Lady* it took Professor Higgins quite a while to transform Eliza Doolittle from a Cockney flower girl to a sophisticated lady who could mingle comfortably with the Royal Society of England. Maybe this is not the best analogy, but in a related way you will start the change from a college student to a polished professional business person, starting with your first job. The development of the nontechnical personality skills should be ongoing and something that you work on throughout your entire business career. It is an essential ingredient for achieving your potential as a professional in the financial world.

What I have outlined in this chapter was summarized in a Gillette razor blade jingle of a few years back—"Look Sharp—Be Sharp." But merely reading about it and achieving it are two different animals—much like reading Jack Nicklaus's golf book might help your golf swing, but only if you have the patience and stamina to put in many hours of practice. In the final analysis, your future job promotions will, of course, be based on performances that are superior and well above the average. In evaluating your work performance, the factors outlined in this chapter are terribly important and can make or break your career development—so don't take them lightly.

Chapter 4

Keep Using Your Crystal Ball

Remember, one of the questions that you are most certain to be asked in your job interview—"where do you want to be in five years?" How are you going to answer? Will it be based on a wish or will it be a realistic goal based on a careful evaluation of your abilities and objectives as you envision yourself in the real world? The question, of course, is extremely difficult because unless you were in an internship training program, you have no job experience or exposure to the environment of the workplace. In my opinion, the best way to go about this is using the technique and descriptions of a strategic business planner as you will read later in this book. You should start by developing your own mission statement—"Who is the real you? What are you all about? What is your realistic career goal?" Here is an example of a *mission statement* that hopefully fits many graduating accounting majors:

> "I am an intelligent, disciplined, and well-liked college graduate with excellent accounting skills that together with continued self-development and at least five years of experience with a Big Six CPA firm, will enable me to achieve my career goal of becoming CFO of a one hundred million dollar company by age forty."

The next step in the planning process is an analysis of your personal strengths and weaknesses. Are your strengths good enough to build on? Are your weaknesses fixable? Having gone through this self-analysis you should then be satisfied that your findings are in conformity with your mission statement. If they are not you should prepare a new mission statement that does conform.

The next step in the strategic planning process is to set forth, in writing, the various strategies you will employ to build on your strengths and eliminate or fix your weaknesses. The final step happens one year later when you take out your crystal ball and look back on how well you carried out all the strategies in your personal strategic plan. You should make a brief explanation on how well you performed on *each* item in your plan—say a grade of one to ten, or if you prefer, A to D—and then give yourself an overall grade for the year as a whole. Then turn your crystal ball around and aim it toward the future. Are my goals still achievable? Do I need to alter my strategies for job troubles that I see ahead? What new strategies do I need for building on strengths and fixing weaknesses? Again, write down your answers, and this becomes your strategic plan for the second year and so ad infinitum. All this soul searching can probably be done in an hour, and I honestly believe it will be the most productive hour you will spend in any year if you go about it objectively. In writing about this I feel a lot like the sinner who has climbed to the pulpit and is now dishing out a fiery sermon to the congregation. Reason? Yours truly was not the best strategic planner in his career. Oh sure, I set some goals and worked on self-improvement, but I did not faithfully make an annual evaluation of the year and where I was headed. At times I fell into the "contented cow" syndrome and would go for a couple of years without an updated personal career plan. This was particularly true during the early seventies when I was in the consulting business. If I had spent that annual hour developing a strategic personal plan, I would have concluded that I should go back to school for an MBA. There is no question in my mind that this would have enabled me to be a notch higher in the financial world, rather than finishing my career as a CEO with Woodhead Industries, a fine but small public company in the electrical industry. This is not a sour grapes epitaph because, as I explained in an earlier chapter, I enjoyed that job. It was interesting, there was enough challenge, and the salary and perks were very satisfactory. However, I am citing myself as an example showing that a lot of competent financial professionals never attain their ultimate potential because they just don't plan their career properly.

In sports, it is a common belief that getting to be champion is easier than staying on as champion. In the financial world there is a similar parallel—getting to be an accounting or financial officer is sometimes easier than keeping the position. In today's competitive marketplace, senior officers cannot rest on their laurels or become contented cows. They should continue to make an annual review and work on their career goals so that their performance, like good whiskey, improves with age. Job complacency is an invitation for trouble, and the last thing you want is to be sacked in the prime time of a career and then face the torture of finding a new job. I don't think that will happen to you if you follow the simple message in this chapter.

Chapter 5

Be Prepared for a Job Change

A very close friend of mine is a senior partner in a prominent corporate recruiting firm. He told me recently that the average accounting graduate can expect to make at least four job changes during their career. If corporate restructuring and white collar employee reductions continue at the present pace, four job changes may be on the low side. Therefore it is extremely important that you be aware of the ever present, unknown forces that will result in a job change and what plans you should develop to minimize the trauma and frustrations of changing jobs.

Let's talk briefly about your first job after graduation. I'm sure you will start your employment with enthusiasm and optimism. But let us suppose that it just doesn't work out for you. What if the job is not challenging or the company is not the class organization you thought it was? Whatever the reason, if you are totally objective in your job evaluation, you owe it to yourself to develop a new career plan that you feel can bring about job satisfaction. Don't get yourself mired down permanently in a job you simply don't like. In your early twenties you have the energy, time, and opportunity to switch gears, change your career path, or even go back to school. If you don't bite the bullet then, when will you? When you are thirty and your lifestyle and family responsibilities make it very difficult to do so? The world is full of successful people who changed career paths after a first job that didn't pan out, so don't be too disappointed if that happens to you. It may be a blessing in disguise. One final observation: in planning a job change, keep working at your present job while you job hunt and interview. Personnel firms all agree that an employed person has a great advantage in the job market over an unemployed person.

As a CFO, I received at least a dozen resumes each week from qualified financial professionals. They were not very pleasant reading, and right
or wrong, I responded to most of these letters, thanking them, telling them
a position was not available, and wishing them good luck. The following
scenarios are typical examples of the job separations that are happening in
today's environment of corporate restructurings and cutbacks in the white
collar group. These are all true.

Scenario 1

A was an honor student with an accounting major who joined a Big Six
firm and became an audit manager after five years. Three years later **A**
accepted a position as controller for one of **A**'s audit clients, a prominent
New York Stock Exchange (NYSE) company located in a medium-sized
Midwestern city. Ten years later **A** was all set to move up to the CFO's job
when the CFO retired at the end of the year. But before **A** could realize this
lifelong ambition, the company lost the battle of an unfriendly takeover by
a corporate raider. Within weeks the new owners of the company brought
in a team of "hatchet men" and fired all of the company's former senior
officers because they wanted their own team. **A** is now jobless in a city
with no comparable job opportunities; **A**'s family has very strong roots in
their community and doesn't want to move.

Scenario 2

B had a similar career as **A**, except **B**'s company won a takeover fight,
and **B** did become the CFO. After five years the company had a "down
year," and its board of directors brought in a new hot shot as the CEO to
turn the company around. After one year the financial results continued to
be unsatisfactory, but the CEO was able to convince the board that this was
all the fault of the inadequate financial control systems of the company.
Allegedly, sleeping dogs were coming out of the woodwork, inventory, and
everywhere, with a disastrous impact on the company's bottom line—in
short the CFO had to go. Out of the blue, **B** was called into the CEO's
office, and after the usual ten minutes of soft words and sweet music, the
CEO hit the guillotine button. **B** had one hour to take any personal belong-
ings and hit the road.

Scenario 3

Following graduation, **C** joined a prominent private industrial firm in
C's hometown as an internal auditor. **C** progressed right up the ladder, first

to head of the auditing department, then assistant controller, controller, and after twenty years, **C** was the CFO and on the company's board of directors. The company at one time was a leader in its field but competition from foreign companies was too much to overcome, and the company fell on hard times and was forced to liquidate. **C** is now jobless in a town where no comparable job opportunities exist.

Scenario 4

D graduated with an accounting degree. **D** was an average student but interviewed well and was employed by a major Fortune 100 company. **D** worked hard but didn't have the brainpower for a senior position. After twenty-four years, **D** had a middle management post, supervisor of standards and variances, in the company's cost section of one of their larger plants. For many years **D**'s company had uninterrupted growth in sales and earnings, but rapid changes in technology and foreign competition brought the company's growth to a halt. With great reluctance, the company announced a massive restructuring that included the severance of thousands of middle management employees throughout the country. The severance terms and conditions were as humane as possible, for example, early entry in the pension plan, generous severance pay, training allowances, and out placement services. However, when the smoke finally settles, **D** is without a job and has a decided shortfall in current income. Worse yet, finding a comparable job will be extremely difficult because **D**'s skills are so specialized and not easily portable.

In the examples above the people were all innocent victims, but unfortunately, they will have to endure the agony of finding new employment. They will have to listen to recruiters tell them they are overqualified, wait for the telephone that never rings, suffer the humiliation of standing in line for their Unemployment Compensation, and many more dehumanizing experiences.

Anyone who has gone through the trauma of finding a new job or a job relocation will tell you it's gut wrenching. I had a taste of it for about two months in the early seventies, when I thought about leaving the consulting business and returning to corporate life as a senior financial officer. The frustrations and disappointments seemed endless—I wouldn't wish that on my worst enemy.

Logically, you might wonder why I am writing about something that may happen many years from now, or hopefully will never happen. Very simply: there are actions that you should undertake when you start your employment that will help you be a better employee and at the same time make it easier to find a new job if you are terminated and must seek employment. The most important security blanket you can have is the CPA Certificate. Take the examination in your senior year, and if you do reasonably well (grades at least in the sixties), keep taking it until you pass it. The CPA degree sets you apart from the rest of the accounting graduates and is highly respected in the financial community. It will allow you to establish a professional practice, and although that might not be compatible with your career goals, it may be the best and only immediate source of income available to you after a job separation.

There are other things that you should start shortly after you begin employment that will enhance your job security blanket. "Become involved in the outside activities of the business you are in."

If you go to work for a CPA firm, join your state CPA Society and become involved with your local chapters, sign up for committee work, write technical papers, and make speeches at breakfast and luncheon meetings sponsored by many business organizations—in short, become a respected name in your field, and enjoy recognition with hundreds of people in the business community.

Likewise, if you're with a corporation, get involved with the Trade or Industry Organizations in which your company has membership—work on committees, write technical papers, and make speeches that will widen and improve your reputation in your industry. Moreover, don't overlook the opportunities to get involved in civic and private organizations like your church, country club, charity drives, etc. This sort of participation adds to the number of important people you know. It is amazing how many of your business associates and friends will help you in time of need.

In my years as the vice president and controller of John Morrell & Company, I was very involved with the American Meat Institute and was chairman of the Industry's Accounting Committee which included a host of prominent names such as Don Kelly, whose deal making with Esmark and Beatrice Foods left a mark in the financial world that still has Wall Street buzzing. After Morrell merged with a New York conglomerate, I declined a transfer to New York and resigned. But because of my reputation in the meat industry I received a number of offers to become a senior officer in other meat companies. After careful study, I elected to leave the industry because I believed its long-term outlook was not good. However, the fact remains that I could have moved into another top position in the meat industry primarily through the reputation and business friendships I developed at Morrell.

As I mentioned earlier, I went into the consulting business a few years later. It was immediately successful thanks to those contacts I developed in the meat industry, and my involvement with civic organizations, my country club, and church. Out of all these contacts, I was able to quickly receive all the assignments I could handle. The income level was quite good, but the cash flow in the early months was a drag, simply because there's usually about a three-month cycle from the billing to collection. This was not a problem for me because I had ample cash reserves for rainy days thanks to lessons learned from my mother, a cash management genius. Her philosophy was "save now and buy later." What a contrast to today's mind-set of "buy now and pay later," and here is an example of what I mean.

Our family survived the big 1929 depression, but in 1935 there was a minor depression that caused some real belt-tightening in our family's lifestyle. When it came time for our usual two-week vacation to Wisconsin, my father's face was solemn and drawn. He announced that there were no funds for the Wisconsin trip. My mother jumped to her feet and with a big grin said, "Who says there are no funds?" In a flash she was up and down the attic stairs, and returning with a big brown paper bag which she emptied—half dollars were all over the living room rug. I thought my father was going to have a stroke, "Marie, what did you do? Rob a bank?" "No" she replied "I saved nickels until I got ten of them, then I changed them to a half dollar. I've been doing this since the 1929 crash." Needless to say we had the most glorious of all of our family vacations, and there was a lot of money left over in my mother's brown bag.

The purpose of telling the story about my mother is to stimulate your interest in starting a program for your own rainy day fund, insurance, and retirement security. One that you should start with your first job and maintain throughout your career.

To illustrate, the good graduating accounting major should start employment with a salary of about $30,000 or $2,500 per month. After getting settled and paying for apartment needs, a new wardrobe, etc., you should establish a monthly budget, setting aside at least ten percent of your gross earnings. This should be done when you receive your paycheck and should be viewed as a bill to pay." (If you wait until the end of the month, there may be very little money left.) A suggested monthly distribution of the $2,500 should include the following.

The Rainy Day Fund

Deposit $100 in a money market account and forget about it. You never touch it unless you're experiencing a job change and you need cash to live on.

Whole Life Insurance

Eventually we all need life insurance, and there is no better time to start than at a young age when the rates are at their lowest. Leading insurance companies have excellent policies that grow in both insured and cash values because the annual dividends are added tax-free to the policy base. These policies also allow for future increases to the policy without a physical examination and a rate change. Moreover, the cash value can always be borrowed at a low interest rate and is another source of emergency funds. For starters figure on $50 per month for this kind of policy.

IRA Account

Currently the annual contribution to a person's Individual Retirement Account is limited to $2,000 per year and may be fully tax-deductible depending on the Adjusted Gross Income level and other factors. Deductible or not, through the miracle of compound interest, an IRA contribution of $2,000 per year for 35 years ($70,000 total) at an investment return of 10% will be worth $700,122 at the end of that period. Can you not afford to start your own IRA as a supplement to your retirement nest egg? For starters try $100 per month.

I would not expect that all readers are going to dash to their bank and insurance company representative right away, but I strongly suggest that you start the above plans by the end of the first year of your employment. As your annual salary increases, you should expand your savings program to include a 401k plan and a stock brokerage account for blue chip investments. Years later you will be very glad you made all of these investment plans.

There is a final bit of advice on this matter of job change. If it is initiated by your company, it is really tantamount to being fired even though they may call it restructuring or some other fancy buzz word. If that happens to you later in your career, remember the following:

1) Throughout your employment, retain notes about your annual personnel reviews and performance evaluations.

2) Don't sign any severance agreement offered by your company until you have reviewed it with your personal legal counsel and received their approval. The courts are looking kindly on dedicated and competent employees who are unfairly terminated.

****

To summarize this chapter, try to pass the CPA exam as a job security blanket for the future, and also get yourself involved in job related civic, professional, and other activities that will increase your reputation and contacts. This will make you a better employee and a better person, and as a by-product of these efforts you will develop into a more marketable professional just in case you must make a job change. And finally, expand upon the investment program suggested so that you can have financial peace of mind throughout your career. When you reach the magic age, you can look forward to a retirement free of financial worries and with enough funds to acquire a second home of your dreams.

Part II.

*Important Financial World Observations
and Accounting Applications*

Chapter 6

The Chart of Accounts—Foundation of a Good System

In all my years of listening to jokes, I don't ever remember a clever joke about an accountant. I did hear a shaggy dog story a long time ago, which is a perfect lead in for this chapter. It's about the general ledger bookkeeper who started each workday by opening a small drawer at the very top of his office desk. He would first look around to be sure that no one was close by, then look over and glance at the contents of the drawer for a few seconds, and quickly lock it. This arcane procedure never changed during his forty years as general ledger bookkeeper. It was to be expected that the office staff had more than a mild interest in that desk, and upon the bookkeeper's retirement, the secret drawer was finally opened by the office manager. "What's in it? What's in it?" The accounting department employees were agog with long-awaited expectations. "Well I'll be," muttered the office manager as he turned over a 3×5 index card. It read: "THE CREDITS ARE ON THE SIDE NEXT TO THE WINDOW!!"

I warned you that this was a shaggy dog story and not a joke, but it is an ideal lead into this chapter because I have dealt with many accountants who didn't know where the credits were. Many times, however, it wasn't their fault because they were working with an archaic and ambiguous chart of accounts, with incomplete and confusing instructions. Throughout my career, I looked at the records of many companies, and far too often I found that sloppy record keeping was due to a poorly drafted chart of accounts. A well-designed chart of accounts that is up-to-date with instructions that are clearly written and understood is absolutely essential to a good workable accounting system—one that easily provides timely, accurate, and meaningful financial data needed by management to efficiently operate the business. Despite its extreme importance, changes and revisions in the chart are often times ignored throughout the year because it can be a little awkward to start a new account during the fiscal year. There-fore, advance planning is necessary to have these set and ready to go *before* the start of the new fiscal year. Otherwise, needed changes might be post-poned for another year.

When I write about a chart of accounts, I am not referring to a standard business form that you can purchase from any office supply store for less than ten dollars. That chart will simply be a listing of typical ledger ac-counts and a suggested account numbering system by standard statement captions—*Current Assets, Fixed Assets, Other Assets, Current Liabilities, Long-term Liabilities, and Stockholder's Equity.* Quite obviously, a stan-dard office form could not possibly include instructions on how each led-ger account is to be used. So even in the smallest of businesses, with only a handful of ledger accounts, there should be clear written instructions on how each account is to be used—When is the account debited and why? When is the account credited and why?

Like all businesses, even the very small ones need their own custom ledger accounts. The corner deli might require "Purchased Meat Inventory a/c," a medical group might require "Patient Office Visits" (filed with Medi-care), and a car dealer might require "Advertising Rebate." This same basic methodology is carried out as well in the mid-sized and the large compa-nies—all require special accounts for their unique businesses. In addition, these larger companies use the chart of accounts as a starting point to take their management reporting system to a very sophisticated level. But to do this, it is absolutely a must that every account in the chart is on a "pure" basis, i.e., the depreciation expense account is nothing but depreciation, the direct labor account is nothing but that—the same for insurance, re-pairs, and every account in the chart.

This may sound so basic that you may be wondering why I am empha-sizing this pure basis. The answer is simple. You cannot write a software program that will print out your financial statements in the format used for reports issued to the stockholders and the public at large if you have a convoluted general and operating ledger. Yet, I came across many compa-nies, large and small, whose general records were such a hodge podge that their published financial reports could only be developed manually after many reclassification adjustments.

The most glaring example was a NYSE Company, with annual sales in excess of five billion dollars. It operated a barber shop in its corporate headquarters, and at a directors meeting, one of the outside directors asked the question of how much it was costing the company for this executive perk. Promptly a new general ledger account "Barber Shop Expense" was established; it was to be charged with salaries, all employee benefits, taxes, interest, etc. Of course at the close of any accounting period this account had to be analyzed in complete detail and all of the expense elements journalized back to the proper account—barber shop salaries to the main salary account, barber shop depreciation to the main depreciation account, etc. There were other accounts like the barber shop, and it all added up to a colossal bookkeeping mess.

Having the data processing department print out the monthly financial statements is a great convenience, but it is not a remarkable accounting achievement—more than forty years ago that was being done in many companies by using punch card accounting machines, and a pure and organized set of general ledger accounts. What is becoming a remarkable accounting achievement, however, is the blending of current computer and software technology and accounting-systems creativity to produce a series of accurate financial reports that are tied in with the general records. These records become a road map to every aspect of a company's business with much dimensional analysis required for management to effectively carry out their responsibilities.

Again, the key to the modern accounting reporting system is a pure and complete chart of accounts augmented by subcodes for every account, which are used to identify and classify the financial data according to the information needs of the company. Every company is different of course, but there are some important reports that are common to all companies such as:

1) Monthly and year-to-date expense centers according to the company's organization chart, actual expenses for the current period compared with the preceding year, and the amounts established in the fiscal year's strategic plan.
2) Monthly and year-to-date sales and gross profit reports for principal product lines or income centers compared with the preceding year and the amounts established in the fiscal year's strategic plan.

Most companies will require similar reports on their manufacturing, inventory, research, advertising, and appropriation activities as well as many more financial reports important to their business. Let me cite two examples from my library of experiences.

As you will see from a later chapter on my Morrell years, the total dollar profits of the big meat packing companies were small, and on a unit or pound basis, seemed even smaller. It was therefore vital to have operating statements that could pinpoint performance in terms of department, product, and marketing profitability. This was achieved through a well-designed system, starting with a good chart of accounts and appropriate subcodes—*Customer Number, Department Number, Product Number, Product Cost, Territory Number, Type of Customer (nine classifications), State (all fifty states)*. By using this system of revenue and expense classifications for *all* transactions, the system provided that the profit and loss statements were automatically prepared in data processing according to:

1) Total plant, broken down by individual departments (pork, beef, bacon, ham, sausage, etc.—about twenty in total)
2) Individual sales territory (about 500 in total) showing individual product sales and related margins and all direct expenses of the sales territory. The profit of the territory did not reflect any effect of plant inventory change or any allocation of indirect administrative and sales overhead, because it would have been a distortion to do so.

Sales were also grouped by nine categories of customers as the economist and the marketing departments needed to follow the trends in the marketplace, i.e., large chains, independents, restaurants, delicatessens, military, and government institutions. The final classification of sales by states was done, of course, to facilitate the preparation of state income taxes. Current product costs were in the system and were updated each week to reflect the fluctuations in the price for cattle and hogs. The sales were margined using these up-to-date costs and the department and product totals were reconciled to the total plant profit and loss statement as part of the normal monthly closing procedures. This customized procedure enabled us to present a "flash" consolidated profit and loss statement on the afternoon of the fifth working day following the monthly closing. At the time, the company had over fifty locations, and annual sales were just under one billion dollars.

Another example of a logical and customized chart of accounts design is still very fresh in my memory. It was that of a leading oil company. Because the tax law at the time allowed depletion on the higher of cost or a flat 27½% of gross income, each oil lease was set up as a separate profit center. Through subcodes, all elements of income and expense that could be directly associated with a lease were charged to the leasehold profit center. At the end of the tax year, the software program printed out a profit and loss statement for each lease using depletion based on cost, and this was used for internal and published financial statements. But for tax purposes, a second print-out was made, showing all the same amounts of income and expense for each lease except depletion. The report would also show the amount of cost depletion and the amount of allowable tax depletion of 27½% of gross income, and then show the higher of two and a final lease profit or loss figure for tax purposes. The excess of percentage depletion over cost depletion would be a *Schedule M* item on the company's federal income tax returns.

It doesn't require too much imagination to visualize how valuable the above information would be to the senior management of Morrell and the CEO of the oil company. In the final analysis, that is the most important key to the modern management reporting system—the involvement and support of top management. Without their guidelines and directions covering the informational needs, the whole system of management reporting can drift to an exercise of futility and a sea of wasted paper. I learned this early in the game, and I always obtained senior management's participation, involvement, and approval on information systems matters. I always found that kind of work both challenging and enjoyable. It was a refreshing opportunity to leave the labyrinth of numbers for awhile and enter the world of accounting artistry. It was in this phase of my business skills where I could make the greatest contribution to the company's success—certainly much more than pure number crunching of debits and credits. In today's business world, the accounting and management information systems design continues to be an ongoing challenge. Rest assured that you will experience this throughout your career.

When you start your first job in the real world don't overlook the importance of the chart of accounts. Along with the usual manuals on broad company policies, accounting procedures, and the company's organizational chart, the new employee can get a quick insight in how a company operates if they take the time to study all of these business documents. This will help you get started on the right foot for your first job whether it be an accounting position in industry or as an auditor starting an examination of a client's financial statements.

Chapter 7

Product Line Profitability—The Heart of Successful Businesses

I would be willing to wager, at better than Las Vegas odds, that most of you were unwittingly introduced to product line profitability before you finished grammar school. The probability is that your first effort as an entrepreneur was the great American tradition—the summertime lemonade stand. In my day, every kid in our block had one at some point over the summer, and sixty years later I don't see any change—the neighborhood lemonade stands still spring up like flowers on hot sunny days.

Back in the 1930s the price of a lemon was only a few pennies, and for less than a quarter you could get enough lemon juice to make a big jug of lemonade holding a generous twenty-five glasses. At 5¢ a glass we would ring up $1.25 and after deducting the 25¢ for the cost of our lemons we were looking at a unit profit of 4¢ a glass and a staggering total profit of $1.00 if we sold all of our daily production. This was not a realistic profit of course, our mothers were only too happy to supply the sugar, ice, glasses, utensils, tables, chairs, and whatever else at no cost. "Only the Shadow knows" what we would have done if we had to cough up another quarter or more for mother's freebies. But the fact remains that as youngsters we were on the cutting edge of learning product profitability. Though it was simple, we knew our product cost and, more importantly, we knew our profit at the end of the day—confirmed by the amount of cash on hand.

Borrowing a line from the musical *My Fair Lady*, "Wouldn't it be lovely" if throughout corporate America the sales VP and the CFO could march into the CEO's office with the product sales report at the end of a week showing comparative product line volume and profitability taken to the bottom line. The proof would be the CFO announcing that the short form weekly profit and loss statement confirmed that the product line profitability was virtually in agreement with the books. This scenario I know happens in some of the best managed companies, but based on my experience, very few companies are able to do this. Oh sure, 99% + companies have comparative monthly and yearly total sales reports and some will include margins and profitability. Unfortunately, when the profit on the sales reports are compared with the books, there is usually a significant difference—and worse yet, the difference can not be reconciled with data substantiated in the records.

Why this concern about profit profitability? It touches the very heart of a business. It is a principal device that continually monitors the entire production and marketing cycle and keeps a running answer to questions like "Should we be in this business? Are we maintaining market share?"

The requirements for an accounting major at the University of Illinois in 1947 included *Cost Accounting I*—only a two hour course. I was fortunate to have Professor Schlatter as my instructor. He wrote the text and was a respected authority on cost accounting. He was bald and somewhat elderly, but had the body and physique of an NFL middle linebacker. He was a kind and jovial man, and when he spoke, his words were worth paying attention to. I'll never forget his comments to us on the first day of class. They went something like this:

> "Most of you are accounting majors, and you are here because this cost accounting course is required. Those of you who enter the public accounting profession will have little need for cost accounting—only to a limited extent on checking balance sheet inventory evaluation. But those of you who go into business accounting upon graduation, or later on, will find that you are exposed to and working with the impact of cost accounting every day. Cost accounting is not a glamorous phase of accounting like consolidations; it may be tedious and boring at times, but good accurate costs are fundamental and needed in well-managed businesses. In the final analysis it enables companies to make the decision on what business they should be in and what product they should or should not be producing."

It was in my third year at Price Waterhouse when Professor Schlatter's words hit home. I was assigned to do an audit of a medium- sized glove manufacturer. When I arrived to start, their controller greeted me with, "Mr. Kurkowski, am I glad you're here. There's something wrong, and I can't put my finger on it. Our sales are at record levels, our accounts receivables are all current, and our expenses are at normal amounts. We've spent very little on capital additions this year, and yet we are practically out of cash." The company's operations were not complex; the prior year audit working papers indicated that the audit was clean except for some inventory work. Accordingly, I decided to concentrate my time on the inventory and the supervision of two assistants who would do the rest of the audit work.

In price testing the major items in the finished goods inventory, I noted that the company had introduced a new line of gloves during the year. These gloves were big sellers, and their material components were among the larger dollar values in the company's total inventory. I went into the cost department and reviewed a bill of material which was the backup for the inventory pricing. Everything on the bill checked out—raw material, direct labor, indirect labor, and factory overhead. But in converting the total cost of a production run to a cost per pair of gloves, a routine clerical error was made (transposition as I recall), and it was not caught by the cost clerk's supervisor. The gloves were priced to the market place on the basis of fifty percent over cost; this had been the company's method of establishing selling prices for new products. In this unfortunate situation, the out-of-pocket manufacturing cost for just material and labor was significantly greater than the selling price of the new line of gloves. So the more they sold, the greater the loss to the company. This quickly explained why their cash had dwindled so much in the current year, and also pointed out to the company a crying need for improvement in the system of manufacturing cost controls. This situation would have been a natural for a professional systems specialist, but back in the late forties the public accounting firms were just starting to look beyond auditing for its professional staff to carry out management studies and other special services for its clients. At the time of this audit there was only one person who was a full-time systems specialist in Price Waterhouse's Chicago office—today the number is in the hundreds.

As I recall the wrap-up of this audit, I made a careful study of the procedures and made appropriate recommendations for needed changes. I didn't return to do the audit the following year, but I learned from my successor that the client implemented my recommendations, and they were very effective.

When I joined John Morrell & Company some five or six years later, I was not surprised to see comparative product profitability reports on a weekly, monthly, and year-to-date basis. The meat industries' selling margins were so small and the competition so intense that it was absolutely necessary to stay on top of the selling performance. These reports were quite reliable, and rarely did the weekly profit and loss summaries add up to an amount significantly different than the monthly statement of net income. Any company in the high volume/low margin business is playing with dynamite if they do not evaluate product profitability currently. Companies with high margins and relatively stable volumes can probably get along nicely with preparing similar margin reports on a comparative monthly and year-to-date basis and similar reports on a weekly basis, only in special situations dictated by business conditions.

There is another dimension of this product profitability matter that is vital and requires comment. It's the possible impact of Pareto's Law. Vilfredo Pareto was an Italian economist (1838-1923) who wrote extensively about statistical theories and methods, and the study of measurement in economics. The formulation of these principles were later applied to business by a number of economists and financial writers and became known as Pareto's Law. I first read about this in the early seventies, and how it was applicable to this matter of product profitability. In essence, Pareto's Law says that as much as ninety percent of the profits of a business are realized from ten percent of the product line, but as little as ten percent of the profit of a business is realized from ninety percent of the product line. The ninety percent and ten percent numbers are guidelines and not absolutes, of course, but this principle was evident in every business I looked at during the last twenty years of my career. The value of this product profitability analysis should be quite apparent. It will highlight the fact that a large number of products in the line are not carrying their share of the load. The expenses associated with a vast array of slow-moving and low-volume items is inordinately much too high, and accordingly, their meager contribution to the corporate bottom line on a realistic basis is even less than shown by the records. Although sales personnel have a great tendency to hold onto sentimental, old product favorites, and also insist that "we've got to have a complete line," it's the well-managed company that will face the realities of the marketplace and eliminate the slow moving "cats and dogs" from the product line.

In this chapter I'm trying to stress the importance of knowing as much as possible about a company's main product. This applies equally to the graduate who starts their career with a CPA firm. When assigned to audit a client, they should tour the plant and familiarize themselves with the production process and final products. Knowing this will be very helpful as they carry out the usual audit work, inspection of invoices, documents, etc. Although not necessary under usual audit requirements, product profitability can be looked into rather easily by the auditor. It is an area where the auditor can indeed render valuable advice to a client on an extremely important matter.

The graduate who starts in the accounting department of a company may not get directly involved with product profitability right away, but it is nearly impossible not to be involved in some phase of it when you consider all the people and departments involved in the manufacturing of a product. Here's a typical scenario. Market research will recommend that the company produce a gadget that works underwater. After the green light from sales and product management, engineering will draw up the blueprints and specifications. Purchasing will order the materials and equipment needed. Industrial engineers will lay out the production line, the production flow, and the associated labor involved. All of this information will be submitted to the cost department that will then prepare a "bill of material" itemizing all of the costs to produce the new gadget. The total cost should then become the basis for margining future sales of this new product. In most companies the cost department usually reports to the controller so it becomes incumbent on the controller to assure that the final costs are accurate, and the expenses and allocations are in keeping with both broad corporate policies and specific company accounting policies. This audited product cost in the bill of material is the starting point for measuring the manufacturing efficiency and product profitability on the sales margin report. This should work fine for awhile, but you can be sure that changes will be the order of the day. Minor revisions in the product may be required because of feedback from market research upon its evaluation of introducing the product into the marketplace. This may set off a domino effect of changes in the entire bill of material, and it is paramount that the systems in place will give effect to all such changes promptly and accurately. This is a matter where a lot of controllers drag their feet by not monitoring all of the data, procedures, and the controls that flow into the bill of material. Over time, the cost on the outdated bill of material is no longer accurate, and as a result, the reports covering manufacturing, efficiency, and product profitability are meaningless and literally worthless. The controller who stays on top of this mundane meat and potatoes accounting will win more gold stars from the CEO than one who lives solely in the world of Accounting Principle Board announcements and the technical accounting rules that are reflected only once a year in the notes to the financial statement in the company's annual report.

One final example from my experiences in this matter illustrates that I have been talking in terms of practical reality. In the early eighties,

Woodhead Industries acquired a small telecommunications company. The timing was perfect because it occurred when "Ma Bell" (AT & T) was split up by Judge Green's historic decision. His order gave enormous opportunities for many small manufacturing companies in the electrical industry. Although this telecommunication subsidiary was a relatively new company, it had state-of-the-art manufacturing controls, bills of material, and indeed a top-notch program for product profitability. This was unusual but fortunate. One of the company's organizers, recently retired, was a manufacturing and cost professional for one of the country's top aerospace companies, and he brought with him some excellent cost systems expertise.

This subsidiary was extremely profitable for about two years and then, as is usually the case, the profit level attracted a lot of competition, which in turn caused the profits to turn downward to more realistic levels. The product profitability report was very reliable and used religiously by management in planning and monitoring the company's business plans. This monthly profitability report started to show profit declines in two fairly significant product groups—one decline was due to volume, the other decline was due to unit margin. A thorough study of the sales and cost particulars of these two groups revealed that one product group was essentially all labor. Foreign competition, using extremely low labor rates, was able to market this product profitably at a sales price that was virtually the same as our most optimum manufacturing cost. The obvious decision was made on this product—discontinue production and consider a private label manufacturing arrangement with the foreign producer.

The second product group was a different situation. The total production cost was essentially all material, and the competition for this product was from a well-established domestic company who had severely reduced the selling price of the product. In this case, our study showed that the competition had modified the product and was producing just as good a mousetrap with a lot less material. Very quickly our product design personnel were able to re-engineer the product using much less material, and in turn brought the manufacturing cost to levels that would allow sales to generate satisfactory profit margins once again.

One of the significant points about the foregoing tale of the two communication products is the fact that the best report in the world is only as good as the people who receive it and use it. All too often top-notch reports collect dust while they rest in peace on top of the credenza behind a manager's desk. In this case good management received the reports and responded quickly with action and corrective measures.

Chapter 8

Transfer Pricing—An Enigma with No Perfect Answer

I don't remember the subject of transfer pricing in any of my classes at the University of Illinois. I came across it for the first time back in the early fifties, during my third year with Price Waterhouse. I was doing some inventory valuation work on the Morrell audit and was furnished a transfer price list that the client used to value some of its year-end FIFO (First In First Out) inventories. In checking the details, I found that the transfer price was not necessarily the actual manufacturing cost or the standard manufacturing cost. It was usually somewhat close, but never the same cost as actual cost or standard cost as shown by computations on file in the company's cost department. "Why the difference?" I asked. "Because transfer prices are not just cost," was the answer. They include many business considerations that management wants included in the inventory value of product that moves from department to department, or from division to division. I then listened to a litany of detailed explanations.

1) The Vice President of Beef believes that the sales departments are not aggressive sellers, and they "give the product away." Accordingly, the transfer price of beef products is the actual cost plus a manufacturing profit. This procedure, the VP of Beef believes, will assure that the division will operate at a profit.

2) The manager of the east coast branches has satisfied the Midwest production plant that the market for smoked hams is very competitive, and the manager needs price relief. Accordingly, they have arrived at a negotiable price of the Midwest selling price less five cents. (A figure that bears no relationship to cost.)

3) The manager of the sausage department, in an attempt to achieve higher sales, has directed that the transfer price should be based on 100% operating efficiency and only 50% of the plant overhead. In this way the manager is confident that by lowering the transfer price to the sales department, it will be able to achieve the higher sales goal.

Some of this may sound a little unorthodox and I don't blame you for thinking that way. But the real world of transfer pricing can be a nightmare, a zoo, a Pandora's Box, and all of the above. Moreover, it can be responsible for poor business decisions that result in significant reductions in corporate net income. Here is a typical example from the real world.

The major meat packers operated huge production plants in the Midwest near the sources of livestock; they also served distribution branches on the coasts near largely populated metropolitan centers. Each plant was a profit center. The smaller distribution branches were at the mercy of the transfer prices, which they were charged by the big Midwest plants. It was no secret that the large Midwest plants gouged the branches with inflated pricing and off-condition product, which resulted in many beautiful branch houses being sold because they continually reported operating losses. Although the losses were artificial and did not belong on the branch books, the price gouging by the big supply plants was done so skillfully that it couldn't be proved by the accounting records. The result was that the company's board of directors ordered that the unprofitable unit be closed and disposed of. Because branch houses were single purpose buildings, they were usually sold at a significant loss.

This was my initial introduction to transfer prices. At first I thought it was a procedure unique in the meat industry. But later in my career, when I held other senior accounting positions and also did consulting work for large multiplant companies, I found the transfer price problem just as prevalent in many other industries. It seemed as though I could never get away from this very pervasive issue. I can assure you that sooner or later, you too will be exposed to it, because the accounting department is usually the scapegoat for transfer price problems and therefore is called upon to fix the problem, even though the controller's department may have had little to say about the methodology for determining transfer prices. Why then should transfer prices be such a problem? The answer lies in the failure of the CEO to clearly outline the company's organization structure and the related rules and responsibilities of management as they pertain to all of the company's profit centers and the flow of any product or asset from one center to another center, as well as allocations of various corporate and divisional administrative expense to the various centers. In this connection, a strong and imaginative CFO should play the lead role in guiding the CEO in these important accounting related company policies. In a company with only one plant, it is easier to control because more than likely the manufacturing departments will be set up as cost centers on a no-gain, no-loss basis. Therefore, the total plant is a single profit center. The problems arise when there are two or more divisions or companies that are in the corporate consolidation, and there is extensive movement of product and intercompany marketing. Which division or company makes the profit and what are the rules governing all of the intercompany transactions? Should the product be transferred from the producing plant to the marketing division on a full cost basis? A standard cost basis? A negotiated price? Full cost plus share of the marketing profit? I have seen all of these different methods and more, but I am convinced that the best procedure is to transfer at realistic standard costs without any special extras tagged on. In other words; if Plant A makes a widget for $7.00, and this is the standard cost for margining widget sales made at Plant A, then $7.00 should be the price that Plant A charges Plant B for intercompany transfers of widgets. In this way the sales margin reports of both plants are on an apples-to-apples basis, and an evaluation of sales performance at the corporate level can be meaningful and not distorted by transfer price "hanky panky." Transfer price manipulations within a company are internal matters and have no adverse legal or tax implications. However, companies who distort transfer prices, which often shift profits to subsidiary companies, are inviting all kinds of trouble from the IRS, who usually look over intercompany transactions rather carefully. Remember this: product movement within a company is a transfer, but product movement among companies within the corporate group is a sale. It must be one of arms length and on a pricing basis that conforms to specific tax rules and regulations.

I thought I would conclude this chapter by highlighting a case history of a proposed acquisition of a large company that was called off primarily because of transfer price overkill on the part of the seller. I am not at liberty to identify the companies or the kind of business they were in, so I'll call the buyer Company A and the seller Company B. I can tell you that both companies were well known, in the same business, and conceptually it seemed a good fit. Both companies operated a number of large manufacturing plants and a complex network of smaller specialty plants and sales warehouses. Company A was strong financially and was known as a good producer. Company B was not terribly strong financially but was an outstanding marketer and enjoyed an enviable consumer franchise.

One of my roles in this transaction was to assemble lots of numbers and prepare a pro forma financial package of what the combined entity would be like after the acquisition. The most important financial reports were the combined operating profit and loss statements on a product basis and on a plant basis. As I recorded the sellers operating numbers, I was amazed at the level of net income shown by their plant profit and loss statements as well as the sales margins on their product sales analysis. When I totalled all of their numbers, my suspicions were confirmed—the total profit was almost double the amount that the seller had reported in its internal consolidated financial statement. When I raised the question of this enormous disparity, the seller's controller explained that the difference was in a "transfer price variance account" carried on the corporate ledger. The genesis of this account is interesting, and another example of how a little adjustment or rule bending can snowball. Here's the story.

The company had experienced a bitter labor strike a few years back. In the settlement the company gave up more in fringes than its industry competitors but despite this, the loyalty and job dedication just wasn't the same when employees returned to work. This resulted in sharp increases in manufacturing labor costs and in turn a hue and cry from the sales department that they couldn't make a fair profit and maintain market position if they were to be charged with inflated product cost. Their point was valid, but instead of turning to a system using realistic standard costs, the company's marketing head, an aggressive tough and dominant employee (also on the company's board of directors) was given carte blanche authority to adjust transfer prices so that sales could show their usual excellent selling margins. The marketing VP was shrewd indeed; he knew that the manufacturing department would scream to the heavens if his transfer price to sales brought about large manufacturing department losses, so he instituted a procedure that allowed the manufacturing department to use a transfer price that would include all of its excess costs and inefficiencies and a modest manufacturing profit. It was like a happy ending to a Walt Disney movie—all of the principal characters walking into the sunlight with euphoric smiles on their faces. But wait! What happened to all those excess manufacturing costs? Elementary, my dear Watson. Those excess costs were buried in a corporate account labeled Transfer price variance. When the company's books were closed, they were deducted from all of the profits reported by their sales divisions and manufacturing plants. This procedure had been in effect for several years, and it truly destroyed the integrity of important management financial and marketing data. It made the postmerger, pro forma operating statements virtually meaningless and became the sticky wicket that caused merger discussions to unravel and finally terminate. Years later Company B went into bankruptcy and liquidated. I firmly believe that its pathetic management information system was a contributing factor to the company's demise.

I have seen major appliance companies buy their motors from a competitor because the purchase price was cheaper than the transfer price from a supplying plant in its corporate group. I could continue on with many more examples because whenever you deal with issues of multiplant, multidivision, and related product movement, you are going to run into transfer price problems. What, then, is the best way to establish workable and acceptable transfer price procedures? As stated earlier, the CEO has to be involved and make certain that senior officers in charge of finance, marketing, and production are all in agreement on the final company policy governing transfer prices. The CFO in particular should prepare pro forma statements showing how the proposed transfer price methodology will work. Moreover, they should review the transfer price methodology with outside tax counsel for a second opinion on how the issue will fly in an Internal Revenue Audit. If the CFO is then satisfied, he/she should review these with the CEO and the senior heads of the production and marketing function to make certain that they are in accord. I've seen new transfer price rules adopted without this kind of careful preparation, and in a few months there were internal wars because someone didn't understand the way they were going to be charged.

That's why the chapter title reads, "An Enigma with No Perfect Answer." In the real world there are *workable* answers, but they will require a lot of thought, diplomacy, and cooperation from everyone involved.

Chapter 9

Mergers and Acquisitions (M&A)—Here to Stay

In March 1955, I left Price Waterhouse and joined one of my clients, John Morrell & Company, the nation's fourth largest meat packer, as controller. I had been out of the University of Illinois for seven years, but the only thing I knew about mergers was how to make the proper accounting entries when A acquires B, and this is something I learned when studying for the 1947 CPA exam. During those seven years at Price Waterhouse, there was very little acquisition activity by the clients of the Chicago office and, unfortunately, I never had the opportunity to work on a single merger or acquisition. This was the beginning of the postwar era, and most businesses were just settling down and regrouping to a peacetime economy. In short, the general business environment was not ready or suited for extensive merger and acquisition activity.

It was inevitable, however, that companies would eventually find many reasons to seek out and acquire other businesses. Among the more obvious were:

1) To increase earnings
2) To expand a product line
3) To add a product line
4) For additional production facilities
5) For diversification
6) For key personnel
7) For technology
8) To eliminate a fierce competitor
9) "Bargains," tax losses, and turnarounds

The pace of merger and acquisition activity started to pick up in the late fifties, and it might be argued that certain sections of the 1954 Tax Code were a factor in the acceleration. The new code clarified the use of tax-loss carryovers and made certain acquisitions attractive from a tax point of view. Merger and acquisition activity continued to grow at a rapid rate in the sixties and since that time has been an integral part of the corporate financial world. Whether you start in public accounting or in private accounting, you are almost certain to be involved in some way with M & A, perhaps as early as in your first year of employment.

Mergers and acquisitions can get started in a number of ways, but more often they begin with the CEO of one company calling his/her counterpart at another company and inviting them for a private lunch to discuss the feasibility of getting together. Before making such a call, the CEO has done some preliminary homework on the target company. They may have done it all themselves or, more than likely, was aided by the CFO and/or the company's investment banking firm who may have suggested the target company. Depending on the size of the transaction, the investment banking firm frequently assists in the negotiations and may be engaged to assure a "fairness opinion" with respect to the final purchase price.

A considerable amount of M&A activity is also done through business brokers who act as matchmakers for buyers and sellers of businesses. Brokers who are able to consummate transactions can earn substantial fees under a compensation arrangement called the *Stayman formula*. It works this way:

> 5% on the 1st million of the purchase price
> 4% on the 2nd million of the purchase price
> 3% on the 3rd million of the purchase price
> 2% on the 4th million of the purchase price
> 1% on the 5th million of the purchase price
> 1% on the excess over five million dollars

So on a five million dollar acquisition the broker can earn $150,000 irrespective of the amount of time or effort. They could spend as little as five minutes on a phone call introducing the parties, or they might work for months in putting the deal together, but in most cases the fee would be the same under the above Stayman formula. Because of the opportunity to make big fees, there are business brokerage firms by the thousands throughout the United States. Many are one and two man firms started by businessmen taking early retirement or who have been terminated from a financial position and are trying to earn a living while they look for another job. There are no professional requirements to become a business broker, so it's not surprising that so many of the practitioners are not more than matchmakers and finders. Of course there are some excellent business broker organizations with a long standing record of ethical deal making. The point I want to emphasize is to carefully check out the organization you may be working with, and after you are satisfied with their integrity and confidentiality, make sure that your understandings and fee arrangements are carefully set forth in writing.

After the CEOs of the buying and selling companies have agreed that there is a conceptual interest in exploring the merits of a deal, there has to be some understanding as to a range of the purchase price. This is where the accounting organizations become involved, because their findings and evaluations will be extremely important in determining a price range for the deal. What does the acquiring company want to know about the selling company?

1) It wants to know its financial operating and marketing history
2) It wants to know how the entire business is currently functioning
3) It wants to know the hidden values that are not on the balance sheet—human assets for example
4) It wants to know where it's going and how well it will perform after it is acquired

The evaluation of the selling company's financial history may be relatively simple if they have clean audited statements by a reliable CPA firm. A meeting between the principals of both companies with the seller's auditors could clear up any points or queries on the historical financial statements. But what if the seller does not have audited statements? Without question the buyer should have at last a three-year review made of the unaudited statements. This could be done either by the buyer's own staff accountants, the buyer's outside auditors, or as is frequently done, by accountants from each organization.

Accounting firms and investment organizations all have a standard acquisition check list, which is a good starting point for the review. It is modified, of course, for any unique aspects of the companies involved for the indicated deal structure. I found these reviews to be interesting, challenging, and fun because they're not just verifying numbers, they're also a study of the quality of the numbers as a means of identifying the strengths and weakness of the business. These reviews are now called due diligence examinations, a somewhat fancier name than "businessman's review" and "horseback audits" as they have been called in the past. Typically the reviews are on a crash basis because time is of the essence. The acquisition process should be done with the utmost speed because leaks will occur no matter how carefully it is planned. Once the leak occurs, the rumors can fly like a wild fire and could be terribly upsetting to the employees and the day-to-day conduct of the business. Accordingly, the acquisition team may work long hours and weekends. However, the nature of the assignment is such that it develops a great deal of camaraderie and job satisfaction. I have never been on an acquisition team that didn't enjoy the total experience, no matter how long the hours were.

It is surprising what you may find when you look over all of the parts of a business during the course of a due diligence examination. Here is an example on how a rote review of the returns and allowance account may produce a very significant piece of information about the company being studied. Assume that annual sales of the target company (a lighting manufacturer) have been growing about 7% a year and are forty million dollars for the current year. Returns and allowances have been steady, running about 1½% of sales. One of your assignments is to review the returns and allowances account and related procedures. You find that the controls are first-rate and your detailed tests of underlying documents and approvals produce no exceptions. However, even though the total dollar amounts of R&A are relatively consistent, your scrutiny of the mix shows some dramatic changes in the past year. You observe a significant number of credits for a track lighting product in the current year, but no credits for this product in the prior year. You investigate. Your findings disclose that this is a new product, and the company was expecting that the new track lighting product would be a big winner in the marketplace—so much so as to allow the customer to return the merchandise without any restocking charge. Unfortunately, the product has failed in the marketplace, because consumers don't like the style. What you uncovered was the tip of the iceberg. More returns will undoubtedly be made. Track lighting inventories will have to be studied for obsolescence and saleability, and purchase orders will be studied for commitments to vendors covering materials and components for the new track lighting product group. Finally, the whole management process covering the development and marketing of new products must be studied to see what went wrong and why.

No two reviews are alike, but a well-executed due diligence examination will discover the main strengths and weaknesses of a company and provide the basis for combining the seller's financial data with the buyer's in a current pro forma statement. Frequently, the purchase price of the transaction is based on the current pro forma statements reflecting current values and current earnings. But in many acquisitions, some if not all of the purchase price will be based on future earnings. This is not an easy task, and no matter how scientific the sales forecast is made, there is always a subjective element in the final number. With this in mind you can see that it is nothing more than arithmetic to work backwards from a future earnings number to arrive at a sales forecast that will work down to the "right bottom-line figure." My experience has been that the sales forecast numbers usually given by the marketing personnel of the buying company are always on the high side. I think that the reasons for this are twofold. First, they are usually optimistic, and secondly, they want the selling company very much and will not submit an unattractive sales forecast and run the risk that the board of directors will turn thumbs down on the acquisition. Therefore the due diligence review should encompass some comprehensive product marketing histories and current sales trends in order to check the reasonableness of the sales forecasts.

We now turn to the magic word that you will hear hundreds of times in your financial career: *synergism. Random House Unabridged Dictionary* (second edition) defines synergism as "the interaction of elements that when combined produce a total effect that is greater than the sum of the individual elements." In short you will hear it in business as:

$$1 + 1 = 3$$

In theory, A's strengths will take care of B's weakness and B's strengths will take care of A's weakness. Now add to this more synergism and "what ifs," and give effect to all these in a second set of pro forma financial statements. These are really the key financial documents in a deal because the board of directors has to be satisfied that the cost of the acquisition is compatible with the impact on short and long term earnings and the financial position of the combined new entity. You can see, therefore, that the due diligence examination must be sufficiently detailed in order that reliable pro forma financial statements can be prepared that are well-documented and clearly satisfy the reasonableness test. Without this kind of quality data, a board of directors would be foolish to approve a deal based on rosy sales forecasts and subjective hopes.

The due diligence examination is quite important from the standpoint of arriving at the best "mechanics" of the deal. In some acquisitions one of the parties may stipulate at the outset what the considerations must be—all cash, part cash and part notes, or perhaps a tax-free exchange. In those situations the deal structure is established at the outset, but in a great many deals the buyer and seller are usually open to details and are willing to let the lawyers and accountants work it out, so long as the final bottom line works out to the agreed upon price. The deal can be made in a number of ways, depending on the financial positions of the buyer and seller, and the market conditions in the case of a company whose stock is publicly traded. Frequently, the findings of the due diligence examinations are critical in developing the right structure. Example: the seller has huge potential liabilities for (1) tax issues raised by the IRS, (2) product warranties, and (3) lawsuits for trademark infringements. Clearly the buyer should insist on the deal being a purchase of assets, leaving the seller to take care of the liabilities. On the other hand, if the seller's business history is excellent and its current financial statements solid and apparently free of potential liabilities, then a purchase or exchange of stock might be the best approach.

One final comment should be made about the all important preparation of the *purchase or merger agreement.* No matter how simple the parties want it to be, the size of the agreement will amaze you—over one hundred pages are commonplace. It's easy to take a cheap shot at the legal fraternity for contract language overkill. However, in today's complex financial society the seemingly endless paragraphs of warranties and covenants are usually necessary. All of the prestigious law firms have veteran specialists who work on nothing but deals, and they are experts at limiting the amount of haggling and nitpicking to a minimum. Sometimes you may have to deal with smaller firms not experienced in M & A matters. Because so much of the contract may border on financial data, expect to be called upon to assist the law firms in writing significant portions of the contract— particularly those points covering inventory valuations, receivable collections, and asset allocations. One thing I can promise you, every contract will have an issue or two that causes delays and incredible hours of haggling before both parties finally agree to the final document. One of my golf buddies, Charles O'Laughlin, a retired senior partner at the prestigious firm of Jenner & Black in Chicago, told me that he's always felt that the best contracts are those in which each party felt they gave up a little too much. After the contract is signed and the closing is completed, it is put in the vault and hopefully never looked at again. With one exception, this was true of the deals in which I was involved. It was a contract in which the CEOs of the buying and selling companies had some oral understandings and agreements on personnel and executive perks, which were not reflected in the contract. Later those matters became the subject of some bitter controversy. Moral of the story: make sure all understandings are reflected in the contract.

Obviously a lot of work is done by the accounting personnel in putting the deal together, but their most important work starts immediately when the contract is signed. Normally a senior member of the buyer's CFO department will be assigned the role of acquisition manager and will usually be in residence at the seller's general office for a month or two, to carry out the terms of the agreement and to integrate the seller's chart of accounts, financial reporting systems, etc., into their company's consolidation. In addition to these matters, they also serve as a clearing house and an "Answerman" for the many questions that arise in the seller's offices in regard to making the postmerger operations run smoothly and in conformity with the buyer's instructions. It is therefore vital that the acquisition manager be a class individual with plenty of finesse in order to help kickoff the business marriage on a harmonious note. The work is both challenging and rewarding, and if you ever have the opportunity to work in that capacity—*Take it!!* You will find it a very satisfying experience.

This overview on mergers and acquisitions would not be complete without some comments on leverage buyouts. Unless you start your employment with an investment banking firm it is very unlikely that you will become involved with LBOs. Nevertheless, I think you should be knowledgeable about them, and I would strongly recommend that you read the book, *Barbarians at the Gate*. The book is nonfiction and mostly about the R.J. Reynolds–Nabisco merger, but it is a thriller that you won't be able to put down. It will not only give you every phase of LBO transactions from A to Z, it will also give you a real world insight into investment banking firms, mergers, acquisitions, and deal making. In case you just don't have time to read this marvelous book here are some brief highlights about LBOs.

They got started in the late seventies as a rather new financing concept in taking all or part of a public company private. This concept was developed on the principle that stable businesses with good cash flows and bankable assets could be acquired with as much as 90% of the purchase price being financed through bank loans, junk bonds, and private investors. The remaining consideration of a scant 10% would come from the deal makers and would be represented by stock, which they in turn would share to some extent with management. The game plan was simply to run a mean and lean operation for a few years and pay down a hefty portion of the LBO debt. Then (if market conditions were advantageous) take the private company public again and the deal makers and management could cash out their stock at a huge gain. This has been done by a number of leading investment houses specializing in LBOs. Forstman Little took MOEN (a leading firm in plumbing fixtures) private in the mid-eighties, and in 1990 sold it to American Brands for a huge profit. Kohlberg Kravis and Roberts (known as KKR) is probably the leading LBO organization. They were responsible for the R.J. Reynolds–Nabisco merger and have successfully cashed out many of their deals. But not all LBOs have worked this well, and at this writing, the jury is still out on them. The heavy debt service requires a steady cash flow, and the dip in economic activity that started in 1990 has reduced cash flow and put many LBOs in a tough bind. That brief recession is quite possibly the reason Congress did not pass legislation to lessen the LBO craze. There had been discussions that some portion of interest expense on LBO transactions would be disallowed. If that tax proposal had been enacted, it would have effectively ended LBOs if the percent of deductibility was significant.

Chapter 10

The Treasurer—Much More than a Money Changer

There are all kinds of unsung heroes in today's world—the offensive lineman who opens up the holes for the all-American running backs who get all the glory; the single parent who works around the clock for their children's college education; and in business, the dedicated and efficient treasurer who makes the CFO look like a champion. In most organizations, the treasurer is responsible for cash, credit, investment, and insurance (now used interchangeably with risk management). Those foundations are extremely important to the smooth and successful operations of the business. They are functions that are accounting related, but not so laced with the kind of accounting theory that you find on a CPA exam. Accordingly, it is not uncommon to find that the educational background of many treasurers is a major in economics or finance and a minor in business management or accounting. The path to the CFO position via the treasury function can be just as good via the controller function. It depends on the individual—as the saying goes, cream rises to the top. In each function there are crossover areas of learning that have to be achieved in order to broaden the total areas of expertise required for the entire CFO function. Therefore, it doesn't matter a great deal where you start in your first job— the treasury side or the accounting side—because in time you'll have to learn enough about both sides in order to administer all of the responsibilities of the CFO.

The rest of this chapter is an overview of the four key treasury functions. It is intended to help you understand the importance of the positions and the challenges confronting treasurers of the nineties. Although you may never have any responsibilities in these functions, I think it is important that you know their inter-workings and tie-ins to the total financial picture.

Cash Management

Cash is the lifeblood of a business. Without the right level of cash flow, a business, like a human being, becomes sick and dies. Therefore, it is the treasurer's highest priority to assure that the company at all times has the cash resources to efficiently operate the business and satisfy the capital requirements for loan repayments, cash dividends to stockholders, new facilities, and investments. In some companies and industries, the profitability and cash flow is so great that their treasurers have a secondary problem within cash management, namely, how to safely invest the excess funds to achieve the highest level of interest and/or dividend income, and for what maturity—one week, one month, or one year? Obviously, the treasurer has to be in tune with the business and the cyclical patterns in cash requirements. (Note: their contribution to the strategic plan will include a projected monthly cash forecast showing the scope of investment activity for excess cash funds.) However, most treasurers don't enjoy the luxury of investing excess cash funds—their task is usually a scramble with the bankers and other financial investors for money. This is where a treasurer's patience and dedication pays off. In today's competitive environment, the major banks and financial institutions have developed a variety of loan "products." It's the good treasurer who has done the leg work on evaluating these products and who in turn has established the right rapport with a number of the institutions whose products best fit the company's needs. So when it's time for a cash infusion, there is no panic. The good treasurer has among other things an established credit line in place, and all he or she needs to do is call their friendly banker and say, "We'll take down a million on the first of the month under our credit line."

  If a company does foreign business of any kind, it is a must for the treasurer to be involved in determining the possibility of foreign exchange exposure. (The credit problems on foreign business are discussed in a later paragraph.) I have seen far too many cases where companies incurred large financial loss because they did not protect their foreign transactions with a hedge or purchase of foreign currency. Whose fault was it? Usually it was the sales or purchasing department who failed to advise the treasurer about the possibility of foreign transactions. It's just another example of the importance of good management communications, as well as the need to cover the foreign exchange problem in the strategic plan so that the treasurer is already alerted of the situation and has done the required leg work to handle the matter promptly and correctly.

The foregoing are some of the bigger aspects of cash management responsibilities. There are smaller ones, and they too are important. Determining the number and location of banks can be extremely important in managing the time that incoming cash receipts are floating in the U.S. mail. Most large banks in the major money centers have worked out programs for efficient cash collection procedures; it's a matter of looking them over and selecting the best one for the company.

The number of banks that a company uses will vary accordingly to its size and location. I've never believed in having accounts in more than two or three major banks with at least one of them having international branches and foreign exchange knowhow. Having just a couple of banks keeps each of them on their toes because you're a good sized account, and you're likely to deal only with their senior officers. If you have too many accounts, you may not be as big or important to them, and you're apt to get the new employees on your account. (That's not all bad, but sometimes this job training gets a bit old.)

The treasurer of a good, solid company will have frequent calls from development officers of competing banks, even though the company's current banking arrangements are satisfactory. I've always felt that on a selective basis, the treasurer should have good contacts at other first-rate financial institutions—just in case.

Obviously, the treasurer is not going to reconcile bank accounts. This kind of nitty-gritty work will usually fall on the newest department employee. It should be a rote function, but cash transactions can become very complex, and all bank reconciliations are not as simple as you might think. Far too often I've seen companies with their bank account reconciliations many months in arrears, and I cannot understand why treasurers sometimes become so lax and forgetful that they don't review them on a monthly basis to see that they are in proper order. The outside auditors rightfully would report this to the audit committee of the company's board of directors, and the treasurer could get a poor mark for something that could easily have been avoided.

Credit

The treasurer's primary role in this important function is to make certain that the credit department procedures are sound and are followed without exception in the day-to-day operation of the company. This means that there is a credit file for every regular trade account, and it contains a variety of data such as credit reports (*Dun and Bradstreet*), financial statements, personal guarantees, etc., all of which are important in determining the credit limit established by the credit manager. It also means that weekly reports should be issued by the data processing department (or the accounting department) showing past due balances and the age thereof, as well as any balance in excess of the credit limit. Although all of the detailed work on credit files, credit approvals, slow pay accounts, and delinquent accounts turned over to collection agencies is normally done by the credit manager and the department employees, the treasurer, nevertheless, should monitor these activities by close contact with the credit manager and by review of these and other timely reports. In theory, a company should never have a credit loss on a customer in excess of the credit limit, because most modern software programs provide for rejecting an incoming order if the order value when added to the customer's present balance exceeds the credit limit. What may happen is that someone in the sales department will okay the rejected order and initial it with some backup notation that seems to justify the credit extension. These rejected orders then find their way back into the system and the order is filled and shipped. I've always felt sorry for the credit department, because if they have few credit losses, the sales department will allege that their stiff credit policies are restricting sales. On the other hand, if the credit department goes along with the sales department's liberal attitudes toward credit limits and past-due balances, it will assuredly lead to heavy credit losses and the credit personnel being in hot water with the CFO and/or the CEO, and in a no-win situation. I've told a few CEOs that their arsenal of management tools should include a peace pipe for use in makeup parties for the sales and credit departments.

The credit zone where the treasurer should be directly involved are all of those risks that are outside of the voluminous day-to-day credit matters pertaining to the company's trade accounts. These would be special transactions such as business with federal and state government agencies, foreign shipments under letter of credit, sight drafts, and security for notes received in connection with the sale of properties. In short, any transaction that ultimately is recorded on the general records as a receivable is the responsibility of the treasurer to see that it is collected in full. In this regard I want to emphasize a note of caution. Today's credit evaluations should not be based on past reputations and/or current hearsay. The increasing number of prominent NYSE companies who have gone into Chapter 11 bankruptcy should be ample warning that current credit determinations should be based on current financial data that is reliable and documented.

Investments

As mentioned in the subsection "Cash Management," the treasurer may have some opportunity from time-to-time to invest cash funds for short periods. However, the principal responsibility in the investment areas will more likely be in the administration of the pension and profit sharing funds. A treasurer may earn their salary many times over through alert and skillful management of these funds. In the great bull market of the late eighties, many pension funds were able to achieve investment performance to levels which fully funded and exceeded all plan liabilities, thereby substantially reducing pension expense, and in some cases eliminating it entirely for some period on into the future.

The usual treasurer's role in the investment performance of the fund starts with the selection of the financial organization that will be responsible for the investment selections and programs. Beyond the selection of the organization, his or her role is to review the investment philosophy strategy and recommendations of the investment advisors and to establish reporting mechanisms that monitor the fund performance on a month-to-month basis. How well investments in stocks and bonds perform can easily be evaluated by comparison with the performance of the S&P 500 (Standard and Poor's 500) and various bond indicators. As an example, pension fund managers may target a performance of 2% or more than the S&P 500 as their goal. Therefore, if the fund performance starts to fall below those levels, it's ample warning that a detailed review of the fund's portfolio should be made. The treasurer is not expected to be a "stock picker"— that's what the fund advisors are paid to do. However, the treasurer should have enough of a feel for the world of investments to be prudent and objective about the specific recommendations of the fund manager. Sometimes the treasurer might have to resort to an old asset called common sense. Back in the early eighties, Woodhead's profit sharing fund was heavily invested in good quality common stocks, but their investment return was running less than the S&P 500. At the same time, interest rates on five-year notes from the best insurance companies soared to 16-17% compounded. I called the fund manager and asked his opinion. He agreed that this was a onetime golden opportunity, and the change over to the 16% notes was made. (As you know from the rule of 72, divide the interest rate into 72, and the answer will tell you how long it will take to double your investment.) In 4½ years, the employees' fund balances doubled, and I was a sort of hero in their eyes. True, that kind of investment opportunity doesn't come along very often, but it illustrates the importance of monitoring the fund performance currently with tenacity and objectivity.

The markets of the nineties have started out on a very volatile pattern and world events appear to portend that continuation—all the more reason for the treasurer to really stay on top of investment responsibility and performance.

Insurance and Risk Management

Depending on the size of the company, the treasurer may be directly involved in all insurance matters or, like the credit function, the treasurer might have an insurance department with a manager and other employees. In either situation, the responsibilities are the same. The treasurer must see that the proper coverage is obtained for all risks associated with the business at the best price available in the marketplace. The employee insurance coverages (group life, major medical, dental, etc.) are usually under the administration of the treasurer's department, although the company's human resource manager may be responsible for drafting the plan and its related benefits. Moreover, the treasurer must continually monitor the company's insurance programs and quickly respond to conditions that bring about changes in the coverages.

Annual insurance expense in the past ten years has escalated at a pace far greater than the country's annual inflation rate. The amounts awarded by juries for damages has pushed premiums for product and general liability coverage to astronomical levels. Likewise, annual coverage for directors and officers is now six figures for most companies, and this is after a healthy deductible. Only a few years ago this coverage for a medium-sized company was under $25,000 per year. The increases in the annual costs for employees' medical plans are even greater and are the largest single component in total insurance cost. It should be apparent that the insurance arena is no place for amateurs. The treasurer must be a professional who can direct and evaluate the entire insurance program. This is usually done through a broker organization that does the leg work of screening the insurance markets for the required coverage at the best price. Establishing the required coverage is, in itself, no easy task. There are many points that have to be addressed. In the case of coverage on tangible property, for example, how much self-insurance (or front-end deductible as it is often called) should be provided? Should the coverage be a replacement value or replacement new value? What about business interruption? For what period? For what amount? In the case of employees medical plans, is it better to self-insure and obtain a stop-loss umbrella policy both for individual claims and aggregate claims for the insurance year? If the company is self-insuring these medical benefits (and that seems to be today's most popular method) the treasurer's department may also be responsible for the review of the claims-processing activity, whether it be done by an outside firm (usually the case) or in-house employees.

Possibly the most important phase of the treasurer's insurance responsibilities is the continuing evaluation of the outside broker organization. Most of the prominent insurance concerns have a staff of technical experts who work with their accounts on programs that can stabilize or even reduce insurance cost. These programs are more sophisticated than the obvious ones like installing a sprinkler system in a building that has an insurance savings payback in four or five years. It is frequently the broker organization that leads the battle with the insurance companies on the settlement of controversial claims. Obviously their work does not end when the insurance policies are placed and the insurance year begins. It continues as an ongoing review of the current programs and the markets, in readiness for next year's programs.

Under the Employee Retirement Income Security Act (ERISA), all companies must file annual reports (Form # 5500 with the U.S. government) covering each employee benefit plan. Since the treasurer's department usually has the cash payment controls for these plans, this department would normally prepare these annual returns. This is a sample of another accounting related activity that goes on in the treasurer's department.

Business Insurance is an excellent weekly trade magazine and is normally circulated in accounting offices. Take the time and scan this excellent publication. Over time you can become pretty knowledgeable about the working of this important financial function.

****

Depending on the size of the organizations, the four functions I have outlined above may not always be under the treasurer. They are very important financial responsibilities, and it doesn't matter if the function is handled by the CFO, the controller, or a different executive. The only thing that matters is that the functions are done correctly and efficiently on a timely basis.

Chapter 11

Strategic Planning Is Not for Dodo Birds

Having spent three years in the U.S. Army Air Force in World War II, I am quite qualified to talk about the dodo birds. If you are not up on Aviculture, permit me to tell you about this ancient bird that became extinct in 1681. The dodo bird looked like an ugly turkey, was clumsy, and worse yet, couldn't fly. Is it any wonder that dodo came into word usage to describe dull, stupid, and simpleminded people, and later, for aviation cadets who had not soloed? When I started my Air Force pilot training at Ryan Field in Hemet, California, it was no surprise that our class was greeted by the upperclassmen with a screaming chorus of "Here come the dodo birds!" We knew that dodo bird moniker would end abruptly in a few weeks when we soloed. WRONG!! Our flight instructors were real tigers, and dodo was their favorite word, which they used constantly when a cadet goofed. The landscape and terrain around Hemet, California, is beautiful, and it was a real thrill to sometimes do a bit of rubber necking and enjoy the scenery below. Major mistake! On a routine training flight one day, my instructor caught me looking back admiring a beautiful array of spa buildings in the San Jaciento mountains. Over the intercom he screamed, "Look where the hell you're going DODO and stop looking at where you've been!"

A few years later I heard the same words, but this time it was not from a U.S. Air Force flight instructor. I was on a calendar year audit of a medium-sized manufacturer. It was early in March, and we were working feverishly to finish the audit and file the tax returns by the March 15th deadline. (Extensions were not requested very often in those days.) The client's president was a friendly man, and he would stop by every few mornings and inquire on the progress of the audit. One morning he greeted us with a solemn expression and in very sobering tones, delivered a short observation that went something like this:

> "Gentlemen, the year you are working on started fifteen months ago and by next week you'll be able to tell me where my company has been. That's fine, but when are you accountants going to tell me where I'm going?"

He knocked us for a loop, and although I cannot recall my exact response, I answered him reassuringly saying, "Someday we might just be able to do that." His initial remark, however, made a deep impression on my business perspective, and it remained with me through my entire career in the financial world. In short, it was the seed that over time made me a planner not just an accountant.

According to one financial historian, the first evidence of planning in American business occurred in 1908 when the board of directors of DuPont required that management submit a business plan for the company. However, the financial world that I saw, beginning in 1948, showed little evidence of real planning. There were increasing numbers of businesses utilizing annual expense budgets and sales forecasts, but these figures were usually guesstimates prepared by the company controller. In the fifties when computers came into being for commercial and business applications, sophisticated planning techniques started to develop. Today the preparation of a company's strategic plan is probably the most important piece of work carved out by top management. You are almost certain to be involved in strategic planning. If you start in the public accounting field, some clients are sure to have a strategic plan, and you most certainly should read it carefully before you start your audit. It can be quite helpful to you in writing the audit programs as well as understanding the figures for the year under review. If the client is not doing any strategic planning, it presents an opportunity for a consulting engagement to instruct management on how to go about it.

If you start employment as an accountant in a large or mid-sized business organization, the odds are good that you will be exposed and involved with the strategic planning methodologies. I'm guessing that small businesses do not have a formalized strategic plan, but I'd be willing to bet that the successful small business with its hands-on entrepreneurial philosophies is doing a lot of strategic planning without realizing it.

The development of a strategic plan requires considerable effort from the CEO down to at least the middle management level. It analyzes and touches every phase of the business. It is not an exercise in numbers, it is a written document that in summary says: "Here is what our company is all about. These are our objectives, and these are the strategies and tactics that we will use to achieve our goals." When these are all in place and approved by the CEO, the final plan is converted to numbers—monthly balance sheets, operating and cash flow statements, and production and marketing data.

The starting point for a strategic plan is a formal mission statement by the company that says who they are, the business they are in, and the company objectives. This sounds like something you could do in half an hour, but I spent several days with six senior officers discussing Woodhead Industries' mission statement before we were unanimously in agreement. You would think that every company knows what business it is in, yet there are many industries and companies who do not know, and who pay a heavy price. Consider the following examples:

Example 1

The railroad industry got into deep financial trouble that ultimately led to bankruptcy for nearly all of our country's leading railroads because they assumed to be in the railroad business rather than the transportation business.

Example 2

Hollywood experienced drastic reorganization because it assumed it was in the movie business rather than the entertainment business.

Example 3

Here is a specific example given by Kenichi Ohmae, Director of McKinsey & Company in Japan.

> "The business definition of laundromats and detergents presents another interesting issue. Detergent makers today, with their large staffs of chemists, see themselves as being in the business of making and selling more and better detergents. But it is obvious when you think about it that nobody really wants to buy detergents. What the customer wants to buy is washing capability. From the user's point of view, the detergent is something that intrudes on the washing process, something that first has to be added and then has to be

rinsed away, with vast amounts of water being wasted in order to get rid of it. What the user fundamentally wants—his or her objective function—is to get rid of the dirt on clothing, not to add and then remove the detergent. A company that does not define its business along the main axis of its users' objective function—in this case, to wash—cannot claim to have a true consumer orientation."

"But suppose a company defines its business domain as getting clothes clean. Then, instead of confining themselves to detergents or other chemical agents, its R&D staff will try to come up with different methods that are within the scope of the company's defined business domain, including such physical approaches as ultrasonic waves. Such a company will not be caught off balance when an appliance manufacturer introduces an ultrasonic laundry machine that requires neither detergents nor rinsing."

I trust that it is apparent to you that the above examples show the importance of drafting a mission statement. America's top corporations think it's important enough to include the mission statement and objectives in their annual report—usually on the inside cover or prominently highlighted elsewhere in the report. Frequently the mission statement, objectives, and the corporate profile are blended together in a variety of ways. Here are a few examples of the different kinds of mission statements from recent annual reports.

Avon Products, Inc.
"Our Vision: To be the company that best understands and satisfies the product, service and self-fulfillment needs of women—globally."

Maytag Corporation
"To improve the quality of home life by designing, building, marketing, and servicing the best appliances in the world."

WMX Technologies, Inc.
"The mission of WMX Technologies, Inc. is to be the acknowledged worldwide leader in providing comprehensive environmental waste management and related services of the highest quality to industry, government, and consumers using state-of-the-art systems responsive to customer need, sound environmental policy, and the highest standards of corporate

citizenship. In fulfilling this mission, we shall provide a rewarding work environment for our people, cooperate with all relevant government agencies, and promote a spirit of partnership with the communities and enterprises we serve as we strive to be a responsible neighbor, while increasing shareholder value."

Amoco Corporation

"Our Mission: Amoco Corporation is a worldwide integrated petroleum and chemical company. We find and develop petroleum resources and provide quality products and services for our customers. We conduct our business responsibly to achieve a superior financial return, balanced with long-term growth, to benefit shareholders and fulfill our commitment to the community and the environment."

"Our Vision: Amoco will be a global business enterprise, recognized throughout the world as preeminent by employees, customers, competitors, investors, and the public. We will be the standard by which other businesses measure their performance. Our hallmarks will be the innovation, initiative, and teamwork of our people, and our ability to anticipate and effectively respond to change, and to create opportunity."

Aon Corporation

"Our mission is to use the skills, experience, and creativity of our outstanding group of professional insurance people, the continuing strength of our financial position and the diversity of our distribution systems to provide valuable and creative products and services to meet the changing insurance and financial services needs of our customers and clients."

Sara Lee Corporation

"Mission: Sara Lee Corporation is to be the leading brand-name food and consumer packaged goods company with major market share positions in key consumer markets throughout the world. We manufacture and market high-quality, marketing-sensitive products with growth potential. These products, which are sold through common distribution channels, include food products, consumer personal products, and household and personal care products."

It's automatic that a complete strategic plan will also include a number of financial goals such as return on equity, annual growth in sales, and net income. This is absolutely essential because it provides the quantified "par" that must be achieved after summarizing the annual plan for every cost center, profit center, administrative, and/or service center in the company.

Instructions for the preparation of the plan would normally be issued around midyear under the signature of the CEO. The instructions should include helpful questionnaires for department evaluations and leave no stone unturned with respect to specific corporate objectives—financial, marketing, production, and research. It should carefully address the important economic, business, and marketing assumptions to be used in preparing the plan, i.e., the rate of inflation and cost of capital. Accordingly, the department heads would have all the necessary tools to go about developing their part of the plan. It means that they must describe its strengths and weaknesses, and present the strategies to correct the weaknesses and augment their strengths. As an example, a marketing department showing a decline in one of its basic products might propose a product redesign as the needed strategy to restore market share. That same department may show that prior-year new products were successfully test marketed in four key cities, and they are now proposing to expand to twenty major markets with heavy store promotions and regional TV advertising. When that department completes its plan, it will include monthly sales volume and gross profit for major product groups along with all direct department and product expenses under the responsibility of the department manager.

Service centers would, of course, have no income, but they too would follow the same procedure with respect to strengths and weaknesses. As an example, the controller's evaluation might show that the department was chronically late in the issuance of the monthly financial statements, and the controller's plan would clearly describe how this would be corrected in the year. On the positive side, analysis might show that a recent conversion of the raw materials inventory records from a manual cardex system to the computer has eliminated one clerk, and it is planned to convert the finished goods inventory from cardex to computer with an expected saving of one clerk. In reviewing the various expenses for which the controller is accountable, he/she might plan a reduction in the annual audit fee because many additional schedules will be prepared by the department for use by the outside auditors.

On a much larger scale, the strategic plan for the research department of a large drug company might be a massive document of a hundred pages or more of dialogue, charts, utilization of many operating expense accounts, as well as requests for capital funds for new facilities to carry out proposed research projects. All of this data would be broken down by individual research projects that would set forth starting and completion dates, as well as the total planned expenditures for each project. Similarly, the advertising department in large consumer products companies would have an enormous quantity of details supporting their strategic plans for each of the major market programs—likewise, its engineering department would have extensive data covering their plans for new facilities, plant machinery and equipment additions and replacements, maintenance programs, etc. In short, every activity of the company would be covered by a strategic game plan. In most organizations, the responsibility to orchestrate the plan from beginning to end usually falls on the shoulders of the CFO and his or her staff. This might vary in different companies depending on their size. In very large corporations this could be the primary responsibility of the director of planning, but they would undoubtedly work very closely with the CFO and his/her staff.

I want to emphasize that strategic planning concepts are not limited to the *statement of income and operations*. They are just as vital and important as they pertain to the financial choices and decisions for the *balance sheet* and *statement of cash flow*. Accordingly, the CFO's strategic plan (usually in collaboration with the CEO) would deal with a host of significant matters.

1) The company's business portfolio—divestitures and acquisitions
2) The company's capital stock—possible secondary offerings, treasury stock and repurchases, options, etc.
3) The level of cash and/or stock dividends
4) The adequacy of the company's long-term debt
5) Investments of excess cash and the important policies affecting the cash position—receivable collections, inventory levels, etc.
6) Important off-balance-sheet items—pension fund performance and adequacy, tax planning strategies, interest rates, foreign exchange exposure, etc.

By addressing all the issues noted above, coupled with the financial data in the operating plan, a complete set of pro forma financial statements can be prepared *before* the company's fiscal year is under way. After approval by senior management and the company's board of directors, it becomes the fiscal year "par" for every unit of the company.

In today's financial world, the strategic planning process has become a standard way of life for most well-managed companies. Its importance is clearly recognized as major companies continue to elect their strategic planning director to senior positions on the corporate management staff.

The American Management Association offers a number of strategic planning seminars. I attended several, years ago, and found them all very well worth the time and effort. If you get the opportunity to attend one, go for it—you'll find it's really worth your while. (It might also bar your boss from ever calling you a dodo.)

Chapter 12

Taxes—Incongruous, Inevitable, Infinitum

Of all the accounting, business, economic, and financial subjects that I studied at the University of Illinois, the one that least prepared me for the real world was taxes. This is not intended to downgrade the curriculum required for my accounting degree, nor the caliber of the instructors teaching courses such as "Introduction to Income Taxes." The very nature of the subject is so complex that at best you can only hope to learn some basic fundamentals that you can build on as you acquire practical experience. It's like reading the very best golf instruction book and then marching to the first tee—you have two chances of shooting under 120, slim and none. After years of practice and experience you can become a good all-around tax man just as similar practice and experience can produce a golfer who regularly scores in the eighties or lower.

The purpose of this chapter is to give you some guidelines and/or a road map to acquire the tax knowledge and skills you will need for future duties as a CFO. This chapter will also be helpful to the graduate who starts in public accounting with the career objective of becoming an audit manager or partner. This chapter is not, however, for graduates who intend to make a career in the tax field either as a tax practitioner or with the IRS. Those graduates would be wise to start promptly on getting a master's degree in taxes from one of the better business colleges/universities.

The history of income taxes in the United States is quite interesting. Did you know that income taxes were first enacted by the Congress in 1861 to pay for the cost of the Civil War? The law expired in 1872, and between 1873 and 1893, sixty-eight different income tax bills were introduced but none passed. In the depression of 1893 Congress finally enacted income tax legislation but the Supreme Court killed it before a dollar was even collected. During the panic of 1907 Congress again tried, unsuccessfully, to pass an income tax law; but finally on March 1, 1913, an income tax law was enacted. The rates were 1 to 7%: (the highest rate was on income over $500,000). The personal exemptions were $3,000 for singles and $4,000 for married couples, and accordingly, this exempted all but the wealthiest families from any income tax liability. From this simple and inauspicious beginning, our income tax laws and regulations have become more and more complex, more confusing, more misunderstood, and obviously much more significant as a producer of the revenues required to pay costs and expenses of city, state, and federal governments.

Is it any wonder that in recent years, complex new tax legislation is jokingly referred to as "the tax practitioners employment act?" Is it any wonder that Washington D.C. has a large population of lobbyists who have been successful in shaping tax legislation that favors special interests and create what we all know to be "loopholes?" As an example, Senator Bill Bradley of New Jersey, a real champion for tax reform, proposed the "Fair Tax Act of 1983." Conceptually it was a fresh, realistic, simplified law that would have been easy to administer, and ended most of the loopholes that had been enacted during the seventy years since the original 1913 Bill. Regrettably, the special interests prevailed, and Senator Bradley's bill never got off the ground. Typically, every proposed tax bill attracts activists with a constituent to favor, or a pet project to advance. Often the objectives appear to be laudable, such as improving the environment, for example. Nevertheless, the effect of these proposed solutions, if enacted, does not simplify the tax code—it only complicates it further.

Since 1983, Congress has continued to pass even greater amounts of confusing and special interest legislation thereby compounding the problems of tax preparation and administration. Here's a bewildering example of what I'm talking about.

In drafting changes for the Internal Revenue Code of 1986 there was a change in the treatment of contributions to College Athletic Programs and Booster Clubs. These are the organizations that give the individual donors game tickets and other privileges related to the school's athletic programs. The new code disqualified such contributions to all colleges and universities except two well-known schools. (These schools were not specifically named but the regulations were so cleverly written that such contributions would only be deductible if made to those two schools.) I can't imagine other members of the committee going along with this one, but it seems to illustrate that much of our tax regulations have their origins in political trade-offs, quid pro quos, and eleventh-hour compromises of the committees who frame the final tax bill.

Gone is the logic, fairness and economic realism that was a hallmark of earlier tax legislation. So much of the changes in the eighties and early nineties have been aimed exclusively at revenue producing in order to help lower our country's annual fiscal deficits. Present tax legislation has deteriorated into a political dogfight, and unfortunately, the elected players in this melee have not been able to draft practical tax legislation that would be fair and realistic to individuals and businesses. The recent regulations that apply to capitalizing petty amounts of administrative expenses as part of inventory are a paperwork nightmare for corporate accounting departments. And yet this new gimmick at best, is only a very small producer of tax revenue. No wonder the tax libraries in the Big Six CPA offices and many law firms are bulging with thousands of books covering tax court cases, history, and explanatory text on all the categories of taxpayers—individuals, corporations, estates, partnerships, trusts, etc. These are some of the necessary tools and references for tax experts who live and breathe taxes as full-time professionals. One of your challenges is to be familiar enough with your company's tax picture so that you know when to intelligently and judiciously engage these experts for assistance.

When I started in public accounting in 1948 it was fairly common for the public accountants to prepare the tax returns for their audit clients or, if done by the client, check it out carefully to the working papers. I had only those introductory tax courses at the University of Illinois, but coupled with the prior year's return's and working papers, visits to the firm's tax library, and numerous phone calls to our tax manager, I was able to prepare the returns satisfactorily. Little by little, I gradually acquired tax experience as I went from client to client. There was another advantage in my early tax work; the tax laws were not as complicated as they are now. Book net income and tax net income were often the same. For some clients, the *schedule M* for differences between book and tax income might include deductions not allowed for life insurance on the companies officers, differences in the bad debt provision, depreciation, etc., but usually not more than three or four adjustments. It was relatively simple to check these different tax rules by stopping in the firm's library and spending a few minutes reviewing those matters in current tax publications. That is basically how I stayed on top of my clients' tax matters. When I was later assigned to audit several companies who used the LIFO (Last In First Out) inventory method I would stop in the firm's library for an hour or so and bone up on what I had to know about the tax ramifications of LIFO inventories. And so it went, as I was assigned to new clients with different tax problems, I would follow the same procedure—go to the library and get the basics.

During those years at Price Waterhouse, I was privileged to do a lot of the work under Ray Hoffman, senior tax partner of the firm. In his day, Mr. Hoffman was one of the foremost tax accountants in the country. He wrote numerous tax books and was always in demand as a speaker. Under him I learned one of the most valuable lessons about the most important phase of the income tax picture—tax planning. How should a business plan its operations so as to minimize income taxes. I remember listening to Ray tell the CEO of one of our clients:

> "First, plan your company's operations to achieve your financial goals without any regard to income taxes. Pretend that there isn't any tax on income. Then let the CFO and his tax advisor study the plan and determine how the plan can be achieved at the lowest amount of income tax exposure."

Too often the impetus and strategies for a business plan are based on tax saving schemes and not necessarily on good business fundamentals. Remember that a company's long range plan should focus primarily on the basic principles of its business, and it should leave the tax planners to orchestrate the legal and accounting mechanics to achieve the best tax position. A few examples should illustrate this important point very clearly.

Example 1

The 1954 Internal Revenue Code included a complete overhaul of corporate reorganizations, mergers and acquisitions, use of loss carryovers, etc. Tax experts saw various loopholes in the new code, and it set off a wave of acquisitions of companies with operating loss carryovers. There were business brokers all over America trafficking in companies with tax loss carryovers and there were small, medium, and large conglomerates ready and willing to buy them. My experience indicated that these deals were usually done correctly, and the acquiror was able to use the existing tax loss carryover. But the acquired company was frequently a real dog and needed untold help from top management. The time, energy, and cost of turnarounds is a terrible drain on a company and unfortunately, the turnaround is not always successful. The bottom line is that the "gain" on the use of the tax loss was more than offset by continuing operating losses.

Years later the tax loss company was divested as part of the new business vogue, restructuring.

Example 2

Many foreign countries have established cash grants and income tax immunity for as much as ten years as an incentive for American companies to build factories and establish a business in their respective countries. For American companies with an ongoing marketing presence, this is an attractive opportunity and has been quite successful for that kind of company. However, I know of a number of companies who could not resist these incentives. They built factories in foreign countries, and even with all the cash grants and incentives, they are losing money on their day-to-day operations as they struggle to achieve a profitable sales level. Presently they still have a tax immunity but they have yet to make a dollar of profit.

Example 3

Not all fifty States have corporate income tax laws and in recent years, as the state income tax rates grew higher and higher, we have witnessed many businesses move their operations to other states. There may be good business reasons for some of these moves, but I have seen a number of operations move to another state solely for reductions in state income tax. How foolish!! The life span of an attractive tax rate can be as short as tomorrow—depending on the mood of that state's legislature.

I don't think I should overload this chapter with more examples. The point I want to make is that good tax planning is vital to the successful conduct of a company's business, but it should always be done in concert with the company's mission statement and strategic plans. At least annually, the CFO working with a tax manager and the tax partners of the company's outside auditing and legal firms should review the company's plans with this group and then decide if any tax strategies can be implemented that can produce some tax savings without adversely affecting the conduct of the company's business. It goes without saying that the same group should meet to discuss any new tax legislation and at that meeting, even the CEO should be in attendance. You may think that you are years away from any involvement in tax planning, so why bother with it now. This is wrong because tax planning is not learned overnight. You have to develop a mind-set for it, and you can do it by staying on top of the overall tax picture by taking a little time each week to read the recent developments and attending periodic seminars on tax topics that are relevant to your company's kind of business. As you develop a feel for tax angles you may spot areas where your company has overlooked some significant tax savings. This is not uncommon because tax laws and regulations are in a constant state of change. I know it's not a picnic to read some of that material, it's gobblety-gook at its best. But remember, nobody said it would be easy to get to the top.

Preparations of Returns

Thanks to the creative use of the computer, the preparations of tax returns today have been greatly simplified. No longer is it necessary to prepare those agonizing spread sheets with their endless lists and columns. Today's software programs, in-house or purchased from outside firms, can process the entire tax return on a per-book basis in a matter of minutes. The only important requirement is that the company's tax officer knows the chart of accounts well enough to know which accounts have to be reclassified to conform to tax reporting requirements and which accounts have to be analyzed for differences between book amounts and the amounts that are allowable for tax purposes. These differences will appear on schedule M which is the reconciliation of tax income to book income. This schedule is scrutinized to the hilt by the revenue agent, and it is important that good working papers are prepared in support of the various tax reclassifications and schedule M items. Likewise, it is important that good working papers are prepared in connection with state returns. Too often companies do a competent job on the federal return and than do the state returns on backs of envelopes. Most state tax laws require the federal return as a starting point, with the amount allocable to the state based on a three-part formula using sales, asset value, and payroll in determining the percent of income allocable to the respective states. Because of increasing state income tax rates it is important that the factors used in determining taxable state income are subject to general ledger checks and are accurately determined and made a part of the working papers for each of the state returns.

One of my wife's Christmas Eve traditions was to leave a tray of cookies and milk near the fireplace for Santa Claus. (I usually took care of the tray's contents by 1:00 A.M., after the children had gone to bed.) I'm not suggesting you give the IRS agents cookies and milk, but I am suggesting that you should be a little aggressive on a few deductions so that the agent is assured of a few adjustments. I'm talking about balance sheet reserves such as bad debts, real estate taxes, and warranties. Despite historic and current data, there is always a subjective element in determining these accruals, and it was with this kind of an account where I would be somewhat aggressive. I might add that my conservative approach was always supported by good data, and it was approved by our outside auditors. These "aggressive" deductions never appeared on the schedule M. They were part of the usual deductions for taxes and various expenses and were "there" if the agent needed something for their quota.

One obvious and concluding point on the preparation of tax returns is that the return should be prepared in accordance with the tax code and tax regulations. You can be aggressive for gray area items that could go either way, but never knowingly hide something that you know is wrong or sign a return you know includes amounts that are clearly in violation of the code. (A $20,000 mink coat given to the wife of a major customer deducted as "promotion expense" would be a good example.) The surest way to a long detailed tax audit is to have an agent find some hanky panky in the return. You can be assured that the agent will turn over every rock looking for adjustments. Moreover, if the hanky panky is serious enough, criminal charges are always a possibility.

The Tax Audit

It is inevitable that the CFO will receive a call from an IRS agent announcing that they have been assigned to examine the company's tax return and are requesting a date that is mutually satisfactory for the commencement of the audit. There are thousands of IRS agents, and in a universe that large, the laws of average will guarantee a small percentage of characters, incompetents, and really tough, biased agents. But by and large, the agents are qualified and conscientious. They have a very tough job and as a group are much maligned simply because nobody likes the drudgery of a tax audit, particularly the conclusion that usually results in additional taxes for the taxpayer. In order for the tax audit to proceed smoothly and without rancor of any kind, there are some common sense rules that should be followed. They are pretty basic, but oddly enough I saw many instances when these things were not done, and it contributed to the detriment of the taxpayer.

1) Make certain that the agent has a private office to work in. You don't want them in the mainstream of the general office where

their presence might make the employees nervous and slow down their normal job function. At the same time the agent would be in a position to see and hear a lot about the business that may cause them to do a lot of unnecessary "exploring" of the company's records.

2) Assign one competent employee to be the primary contact with the agent. That employee should be responsible for delivering or preparing the documents requested by the agent. In turn, that employee should keep a record or copy of everything turned over to the agent. Provide the agent with any reasonable request for information, but don't give them a hunting license to fish through the records.

3) Treat the agent as a professional. Always call them Mr. or Ms. and don't become buddy-buddy with them. Entertaining the agent with lunch and any kind of favors should be out of the question.

4) As the audit proceeds, the agent undoubtedly will raise a number of questions, or disagree with certain amounts. The company's primary contact (with behind-the-scenes guidance from the boss) should respond to these matters, but he/she should not agree or settle any of these issues. These should all be reviewed at the wrap-up of the audit between the agent and the company tax officer. At this session, a lot of horse trading and compromise usually takes place and hopefully a reasonable settlement can be agreed upon. Then it is time to contact your outside tax counsel for advice on whether to settle or fight the issues in question, and how far—all the way to tax court?

Although an audit by a state income tax agent is usually very brief (only a day or two), the same common sense rules stated above should likewise be followed.

Tax Provisions and Tax Reserves

The provision for income taxes and the adequacy of the tax reserves is no longer a simple calculation in the preparation of a company's annual financial statements. The Statement of Financial Accounting Standards No. 109, "Accounting for Income Taxes," which became effective in 1993, requires that the note to their financial statements for income taxes, includes tabulations for the current year and the two preceding years of:

1) Tax provisions according to domestic and foreign operations
2) Reconciliation of the statutory tax rate to the effective tax rate
3) Components of the tax provision by taxing jurisdiction (federal, foreign, and state) according to current taxes and deferred taxes
4) Temporary differences and carryforwards which give rise to deferred tax assets and liabilities

These financial tabulations and accompanying text require as much as two full pages in the "notes to the financial statements." To finally arrive at accurate numbers is an ongoing evaluation of complex financial data. In my opinion, the only way to achieve this is to set up separate working papers for every piece of the puzzle. That means that in addition to the federal tax working papers, separate papers should be prepared and maintained for every state and foreign country where the company is required to file returns. The financial data in these papers must also be classified according to current taxability as well as the amount and kind of data subject to deferred taxability. When this is done correctly, it is only a matter of multiplication to compute the tax provisions for the current year. These same working papers will also provide the basis for determining the needed tax reserves for the open years, usually the past three years unless a waiver has been signed for earlier years. In the absence of good working papers, companies have used shortcuts in this matter of tax provisions and reserves, such as using historic averages for data used in deferred taxes, or cash basis accounting for state tax payments. Over time, such practices are bound to result in some serious misstatements of these key tax figures. My other suggestion on this matter is the need for the company's tax personnel to work closely with the company's independent auditors on the preparation and maintenance of the suggested working papers, and to have a continuing dialogue on all the data that affects them, including Internal Revenue audit adjustments, which will impact virtually every state return for open years. This kind of rapport is good insurance against year-end surprises in a company's tax accounts and will also hold down the audit fee pertaining to the review of the tax provision and tax reserve.

After-Hours Tax Advice

It's only a matter of time until your friends and relatives know that you are a financial professional. If you have your CPA certificate, they firmly believe that you have all the answers to any financial investment or tax question. I can assure you that human nature being what it is, you will always have people asking you for free tax advice at cocktail or dinner parties, at the nineteenth hole, etc. Let me now give you some good advice on this.

"Never give any definite answers to their questions"—you have nothing to gain and everything to lose. You can still be very sociable and discuss their problems briefly but in such a general way that you haven't lost your professionalism by practicing your skills at cocktail parties for free. What you should have handy, is a number of your own escape phrases that you can use when the situation presents itself. Medical doctors have a good way of handling similar situations. They tell their fellow dinner guest to call their office for an appointment, as they would be pleased to see them about their medical problems.

****

The world of income taxes is no fun. The rules are in a continual state of change and in many ways are not equitable or compatible with good business practices. Nevertheless, all individuals and business organizations have to live with these rules that will require tax payments of a significant portion of their annual income. In the case of most corporations, the combined federal, state, and city income taxes is now over fifty percent. Within that framework, effective tax planning in some cases can ease the annual tax burden without jeopardizing the good conduct of the business. This is the ongoing challenge of financial officers and the creative tax professionals in principal CPA and law firms. The skills of these experts are not learned overnight. It is the result of continuing study, observation, and involvement in the total tax environment. Tax preparation and tax audits are important components of the total tax picture. These functions require endless hours of detailed work, research, and above all, patience and dedication. Just more reasons why taxes aren't much fun, though they are an important business discipline we financial professionals all have to live with.

Chapter 13

Taking Care of Inventories

If you select a hundred annual reports at random you will find that the inventory balance is usually the first or second largest asset on the balance sheet. If you keep a watchful eye on *The Wall Street Journal* you will read that inventory write-downs are often given as the reason for year-end surprises that cause sharp decreases in earnings (and in some cases, the primary reason for a Chapter ll bankruptcy announcement). If you talk to leading commercial lenders you will find that they frequently will accept as little as thirty percent of a business's inventory value as loan collateral. Inventories are potentially the "cesspool of the balance sheet," and in my opinion, one area of the business where corporate management generally has not done a good job.

Many departments within a company can be responsible for major inventory problems—engineering and/or product design, purchasing, industrial engineering, sales and marketing, and of course, accounting. In the final analysis, the inventory adjustment is basically two-sided—the physical side on the factory floor and the record keeping side in the controller's department. As accountants, you can surely do something about the record keeping, and perhaps also help solve inventory problems on the factory floor, or improve the procedures covering departments such as engineering or purchasing, whose involvement with production has significant effects on inventories.

The quantity problems that surface on the taking of a physical inventory are usually a combination of slow moving or excess stocks, obsolete items, and defective items. All of these items are candidates for write-offs, but the question is whether management will bite the bullet and recognize it in their financial statements, or develop a rationale justifying its full value along with the expectation that it will be sold within the ensuing year, thereby meeting the requirement for its classification as a current asset.

Inventory valuation problems can also come to light in the pricing of the year-end inventories. Normally these adjustments are the result of errors in recording the correct purchase price of materials, compounded by incorrect amounts for labor and overhead included in the total inventory cost. In a big inventory there is bound to be a few errors of this nature, but the dollar effect should not be material. A large pricing adjustment is inexcusable and clearly indicates a serious breakdown in some phase of the inventory procedures.

My experience with huge inventory write-offs was that they did not suddenly develop in a current year. Looking at the genesis of the write-offs, it usually spanned a period of several years, and there was always some justification for management's position despite more compelling reasons for a write-off. One reason for not biting the bullet is the impact of a historic inventory tax case a few years back involving the Thor Power Company. That company had established a large reserve for obsolete inventory and claimed the inventory write-down on its tax return. However, it did not physically dispose of the obsolete inventory but kept it on hand for possible future use. The tax court held that the deduction was not allowable because the company did not dispose of the inventory. Hence, the obvious reluctance on the part of management to dispose of inventory that "may" have had future use. Indeed it is a situation that is truly between a rock and a hard place on some of the year-end inventory decisions.

It is inherent to find human errors in business; marketing might overestimate the sales forecast, engineering's new product will have a design flaw, purchasing will overbuy, etc. These are the kinds of events that cause slow-moving and obsolete stock. However, their adverse impact on profits can be minimized with good inventory management and a constant watchful eye on inventory turnover. The Japanese management technique of "Just-in-time (JIT) Inventory" has resulted in astounding reductions in inventory levels and corresponding increases in turnovers. This inventory concept has found widespread use in American business. Its proliferation cannot come soon enough to improve the overall financial health of our country's manufacturing companies.

The foregoing paragraphs touched on some of the inventory problems associated with the production and marketing of a company's product. What about inventory problems and adjustments that are accounting related and are the responsibility of a chief accounting officer. As far as the board of directors is concerned, adverse year-end inventory adjustments of any kind are usually associated with accounting personnel even though the bulk of the adjustment may be the fault of errors in another department. I am generally in support of the principle, since the chief accounting officer is responsible for establishing and maintaining effective inventory procedures, and monitoring the activities of the related departments whose performance and financial data have a significant and direct bearing on book inventory balances. The controller therefore should be responsible for inventory adjustments. The controller, who at the beginning of the fiscal year establishes standard journal entries for monthly cost of sales, variance accounts for materials, labor, overhead, etc., and who remains at a desk like a Sitting Bull for the next twelve months is asking for trouble. If there is a year-end inventory disaster, that controller can only blame themself if they receive a pink slip from the Board. This may sound like I'm coming down pretty hard on the controller whose company has a big year-end inventory surprise. Staying on top of inventories is one of a controller's most important responsibilities and probably the most difficult because they must deal with a host of nonaccounting data that are generated outside of the accounting department. While these various plant operating activities can have significant effects on inventory balances, my forty years of experience clearly shows that the biggest year-end inventory adjustments are caused by *inaccurate monthly cost of sales entries.*

Inaccurate Monthly Cost of Sales Entries

Usually the error is due to using costs lower than the actual in the costing of the monthly sales. This has the result of producing phantom profits and an inflated book inventory. When the physical inventory is taken and priced, the beautiful profit picture is turned very ugly by a whopping adjustment to write down the inventories. Management and the financial community perceive these write-downs as inventory adjustments; technically, they are cost of sales adjustments, the responsibility for which is the chief accounting officer. The senior management of companies with a historic pattern of huge year-end inventory adjustments work in fear during the twenty to thirty days it usually requires for the taking, valuation, and determination of the final year-end inventory adjustment.

There are a number of other observations about this inventory matter that I want to leave you with.

Observation 1

Inventory procedures and systems are as unique as a human finger-print—no two are alike. I recall in my role as the chairman of the American Meat Institutes Accounting Committee that we attempted to accumulate industry-wide statistics on the hog slaughtering operation for purposes of evaluating hog marketing and buying performance as well as a measurement of the operating expenses in that one department. We were amazed when we received the numbers from the reporting companies—to put it bluntly, the figures on an apples-to-apples basis were cockeyed. After a lot of effort, my committee was able to reconcile the reported figures and overcome the lack of comparability caused by wide differences in each company's inventory and plant operating practices.

Observation 2

Physical inventories that are taken only once a year are the worst kind, simply because the employees taking the inventory are obviously rusty and if a lot of calculations are required, the typical plant employee is not usually blessed with needed mathematical skills. Moreover, written inventory instructions are rarely as complete as they should be, the number of plant supervisors are never enough, and the personnel from the company's independent CPA firms who are present to observe the inventory are relatively inexperienced—first and second year juniors. The solution is an obvious one—design the inventory system so that physical inventories are taken on a cycle basis throughout the year by an experienced physical inventory team. This is the way it's done in top-notch companies and is close to a fool proof method of avoiding a possible large inventory adjustment for a physical inventory taken in its entirety only at the end of the company's fiscal year.

Observation 3

The system of inventory procedures, beginning with the procurement of materials and the production and shipment of finished goods, should be designed to mirror these functions in the general ledger so that they are all subject to the check and balance of financial controls. One of the most important controls covers the order, shipping, and billing functions, and it should be so airtight that there is 100% assurance that everything that leaves the plant is either billed to a customer or accounted for by a general ledger entry for the item—i.e., inventory consigned to warehouses or salesmen, product sent to a supplier for further processing, samples, etc. This kind of control virtually guarantees the validity of the credit to the finished goods inventory computed from the monthly shipment report.

It should be apparent that the whole inventory process and related functions is one of the most complex parts of a company's accounting system. It is a high priority challenge for the chief accounting officer to be creative and establish a system of financial and management controls over what is the "guts of the business." As the chief accounting officer, he/she may have inherited a system that is thirty years old and literally processed on the backs of envelopes, but like they say: "If it ain't broke—don't fix it." On the other hand, the chief accounting officer may have inherited what appears to be a dream system—everything is on-line, and beautiful management reports are being cranked out in colored graphs by today's high tech office devices. Yet the operations are a disaster, key materials are out of sync, sales is crying for certain hot items and the finished goods warehouse is bulging with slow moving merchandise. Is this make-believe? Not really. I've seen plenty of inventory accounting systems that looked good only on paper. It did not properly interface with what was really happening in the business. So, I leave you with this final thought. No matter where your career path takes you in accounting—CPA manager or partner, or CFO or controller in business, always keep your eye on this inventory matter because it is the one place where Murphy's Law is always lurking. But remember, keeping your eye on the inventory also means that you look through the inventory system and see all the business functions operating, and when those functions change, you must modify your inventory systems to accommodate the change.

A chapter on inventories would not be complete without commentary on the LIFO method for the valuation of inventories. The accounting profession had approved this method for years because it matched current costs with current revenue, with the result that paper profits were not created by inventory appreciation. Around 1940 the Internal Revenue Service allowed LIFO for tax purposes and accordingly a great many companies have adopted the LIFO method because of the favorable impact on cash flow and lower income taxes. The LIFO method is very complex and must conform to detailed IRS regulations. Accordingly, it is not practicable to calculate an *exact* LIFO reserve at each monthly closing, but it is possible to establish fairly accurate monthly adjustments to the LIFO reserve. This can be done by a study of the historic inventory patterns and correctly incorporating expected current year changes in the mix and price level, and whether there will be increments or decrements in either inventory dollars or quantities. In this connection it is important to point out that additional profits can be realized because of year-end inventory changes that result in a liquidation of lower priced LIFO inventory quantities. If the amount is material, the auditors may require disclosure in the inventory note to the financial statements, but sometimes this is so buried that it usually goes unnoticed and is quickly forgotten about in the financial community. Most of the favorable inventory windfalls observed in annual reports are the result of legitimate changes in a company's business and/or product changes that cause the liquidation of low-priced LIFO inventory. That's fine, but it is poor business judgement when a company deliberately manipulates its year-end inventories so that it can rob its LIFO reserve and improve reported profits. That is a classic example of a "pyrrhic victory" because the increase in reported profits is at the cost of an unnecessary increase in the company's Federal Income Taxes.

Chapter 14

Today's Board of Directors—Good Old Boys Revisited?

When I entered the financial world in February of 1948, my perception and understanding of a board of directors was quite limited. Their role and purpose was touched on lightly in a required business management course at the University of Illinois, and the closest I ever came to a board room was seeing one in an old British movie. During my first six years at Price Waterhouse, I had no direct contact whatsoever with any corporate board or any committee of the board. In those days the auditors rarely met with the board, and if they did, it was a partner who would represent the firm. However, as a staff member in charge of the field work, I had plenty of indirect contact with the boards of all my clients via the inspection of the *Corporate Minute Book*. As you would expect, the *Minute Book* contains the resolutions and approvals of a number of routine business matters, such as opening and closing of bank accounts, election of officers, declarations of dividends, capital budget, and purchases and sales of major investments. As an auditor, my primary focus was on the matters that pertained to the company's financial statements. My secondary focus was on the highlights of discussions pertaining to current operations and future plans, which some companies include in their board minutes. While I did not have the business experience or knowledge to understand all of the subtleties of the board room, this information was put to good use in planning the audit to encompass matters that were of concern at the board level.

My first direct contact with any board of directors came right out of the blue. I was down the home stretch on the Morrell audit which had gone very smoothly with the exception of an unusual LIFO inventory adjustment caused by a temporary liquidation of part of their LIFO base. The company's fiscal year was October 31 (traditional for major meat packers), but their tax year was December 31, which was established to coincide with changing patterns in livestock marketing and inventory requirements. The problem was to compute a LIFO reserve at October 31 for liquidated inventories that would not be replaced until December 31. There were many variables—fluctuating livestock prices, product mix, and alternative product sources. In short, it was a very complicated accounting problem with several possible approaches and solutions. It was mid-morning; I was going full steam ahead, buttoning up the audit when the CEO's secretary stopped at my desk and said "Mr. McCallum (the CEO) wants you in the board room; bring your LIFO papers." Sure enough, the board room was just like the old British movie—distinguished elderly men in their late fifties (I was only thirty at the time) sitting around a huge handsomely carved oak table in a room with exquisite wall coverings, appointments, and of course, impressive oil paintings including portraits of the company's founders and earlier chairmen. The board members were very cordial, but also very serious and businesslike. I was on center stage for about half an hour explaining the LIFO problem and fielding their questions, which were constructive and well thought out. It was a confidence building experience to say the least. I left the room thinking, "It might be pretty neat to be a director some day."

What about you? Are you going to be meeting with the board or committees of the board? The answer is yes, if you start your career with a company whose stock is publicly traded or with a large CPA firm whose audit clients include a large number of public companies. Either way, you will undoubtedly attend meetings of the audit committee of the board, and typically that committee will meet three times during the company's fiscal year. The first meeting is to review and approve the plan and scope of the audit work proposed by the company's outside auditors. The remaining two meetings are held after the auditor's sign-off date. One of the meetings deals with the financial statements and the fiscal year-end report, and the other, held at a later date, addresses internal controls, procedures, and business suggestions that the auditors developed during the course of their work. At all of these meetings the committee will meet jointly with members of the outside auditing firm and the CFO's staff, but the committee will also meet separately with the auditors to hear their opinions on the quality of personnel and work carried out by the CFO's organization. Likewise, the committee will meet separately with the CFO's staff to obtain their opinions on the quality and effectiveness of the personnel from the outside auditing firm. Since the mid-seventies, regulatory agencies such as the

Securities Exchange Commission (SEC) and NYSE have required that audit committees be composed solely of outside directors. Having been an outside director at Woodhead Industries for several years, I was chairman of the audit committee during that period, and I can assure you that the audit committee meetings are among the most important held by any board committee. When you are asked to attend one of these meetings, remember to be well-prepared and conduct yourself like a real professional. The chairman of the audit committee will give a report of these meetings to the full board, and it is important in your career development to leave lasting good impressions with the company's board of directors. Moreover, if you become a controller, treasurer, or CFO, you are certain to be included in many meetings of your company's full board. That was my experience at John Morrell & Company. Though I was not a member, I attended nearly every meeting of the board during my thirteen-year tenure. This was a very valuable experience for me, which I put to good use when I went on a number of boards later in my career.

When I finished college in the mid-forties and went into the business world, the man-on-the-street perception of a board of directors was that it was a group of the company president's friends that would meet a few times a year for a review of the company's business, followed by a nice lunch at the president's club during which the president's secretary would distribute some crisp new currency to each director for the meeting fee. Along the way, some journalist or financial writer coined the phrase "good old boys" as the description and connotation for those boards loaded with cronies of the president that would rubber stamp any meeting agenda. Perhaps this was true to an extent, but how pervasive, is anybody's guess. In any event, the term "good old boys" stuck and is used frequently in today's financial press.

Today's boards of directors are a lot different than those back in the forties—there are more outside directors, there are many more board committees, and the annual director fees and perks have increased to very hefty levels. By the same token, today's boards have a lot more challenging issues to deal with—increased merger and takeover activity, "poison pill" strategies, deferred executive compensation plans, stock option plans and golden parachutes, proxy fights, EPA issues and restructurings, etc. Reporting on these very demanding board level matters was usually found only in the financial press, but the magnitude of these matters has reached levels of national importance and are frequently on the front page of the daily newspapers and featured on nightly television and radio newscasts (example: the late 1992 financial nightmares and restructuring of General Motors and IBM). This new focus on the role of corporate boards has raised many questions in financial circles throughout corporate America about the role of directors and the overall capability and effectiveness of the corporate board of directors. As we learned about the financial debacles in our savings and loan industry, massive corporate restructurings, and more Chapter 11 bankruptcies, this question is heard time and again—"what were the directors doing when all this was going on?"

The reaction to this has been a lot of director bashing in the financial press. Here is a typical example excerpted from the May 22, 1995, *Forbes* story, "The cosseted director."

> "Big corporations have been showering more and more goodies on their boards of directors...Today the average pay of directors of the 200 largest industrial companies in the U.S. is $68,300, according to compensation consultants Pearl Meyer & Partners. This works out to about $700 an hour, far more than leading corporate lawyers are getting."
>
> "...the lavishness of some of today's directorship perks raises troubling questions. A board of directors is supposed to represent the interests of shareholders. It is supposed to keep its collective eye on management, giving it advice, even when unwanted, prodding it when necessary and, in extreme cases, kicking it out...How motivated can a board be to get tough with the CEO when that chief executive showers it with goodies?" "Is it any wonder some of these boards have dithered in the face of obvious mismanagement?"
>
> "It's the last dirty secret. Directors taking large sums of money, but holding...few shares in the companies they're serving." (Dana Wechsler Linden and Robert Lenzner with Frank Wolfe, "The cosseted director," *Forbes*, 22 May 1995, 168-170.)

I would like to think that the above report is not representative of most corporate boards. Based on my experiences, it is not. In my forty years in business I saw a few "rubber stampers," self-centered board misfits, and the like, but by and large the vast majority of my board experiences were with people who were capable, dedicated, and who believed they always acted in the best interest of the stockholders. I do think, however, that there is sufficient concern about many aspects of the role of directors and functions of the corporate board, and in due course changes will be made by Congress, the NYSE, or the SEC. I can safely predict that when the 1996 college graduates start to become directors, the corporate board of today will be nowhere in sight.

When all of its responsibilities, powers, and ramifications are placed side by side, the corporate board of directors becomes a tremendously complex institution. This chapter only scratches the surface, and I would suggest you plan to read *Handbook for Corporate Directors* by Mattes and Ball. It is an excellent book—sixty-one chapters in all, authored by top people from academia, business, and the investment community. It covers all important aspects of the working of a board of directors.

The corporate form of business organization and ownership has been around for a long time. Some historians say it started with the Code of Hammurabi in 2083 B.C. with the Babylonians carried on to the Greek and Roman civilizations, and finally, arrived in England, where in the sixteenth century they added the concept of a governing board of directors. Not surprisingly, these business practices came to America during its colonization by the English, and "the first general corporation law for business purposes is commonly credited to the state of New York in the year 1811." [Miles L. Mace, *Directors: Myth and Reality* (Boston, MA: Division of Research, Graduate School of Business Administration, Harvard University, 1971), 6.]

Obviously, the corporate structure with its governing board has stood the test of time, and its concept has been vital in providing an important means for business continuity, investment, and ownership. However, I do believe that some controls and changes are needed in order to assure the integrity and continuing satisfactory performance of corporate boards. I am not alone in this observation. The following is from Waldo's, *Boards of Directors*:

> "A Bleak View of the Board"
> "Despite the best intentions of hard-working outside board members, some observers of the board scene take a pretty pessimistic or cynical view of their ability to make a genuine contribution to effective operations. No less a personage than noted consultant, author, and teacher, Peter Drucker feels that there is no evidence to support the theory that boards really do govern and even matter. He says:
>
> > 'Life on the board is not juicy or exciting. Rather, it is dull. Board members are more often bored by routine than stimu-

lated by manipulating the levers of power. . . . Some board members, aware of their powerlessness, are beginning to complain that they serve no function and are kept busy with trivia, even when they want to do serious work. . . If boards are to function with a serious purpose, some major changes are needed.'

Drucker then goes on to describe some of the unhappy experiences he has had serving on several boards—so unhappy in fact, that he now refuses to serve on any board." [Charles N. Waldo, *Boards of Directors: Their changing roles, structure, and information needs* (Westport, CT: Quorum Books, 1985), 14.]

I don't know precisely the changes Mr. Drucker had in mind, but I would like to see several changes in the nominating and director election procedures for publicly held companies. Presently, the CEO handpicks who goes on and off the board. I know there is a special nominating committee of the board who theoretically makes the selections, but let's face it, CEOs control the company, and they control the board. Realistically, the shareholders have nothing to say about who goes on the board. All they can do when they receive their proxy statement is either approve the management slate, not vote at all, or withhold their vote—practically speaking, a worthless exercise. I believe the major stockholders should have a committee that could elect a director, and I also believe that a similar procedure be given to the employees so that they too could elect a director. Who has a greater stake in the operations and future of a company than its owners and employees? Why then should they be denied *direct* representation on the board? After all, aren't the chances for success greater when the three groups, directors, owners, and employees, are better informed and work as a team to achieve common goals.

I have one more idea that may sound a little picky. Namely, place a reasonable restriction on the so called "professional directors" as to the number of public company boards they can serve on. From a social point of view, I don't think it is in the best interest of our country when a hundred or so individuals sit on as many as four and five boards of S&P 500 companies. Moreover, I wonder how effective they can be wearing that many hats.

I hope I have given you enough food for thought to stimulate your interest in following the changes and the involvement of the boards of directors' role in our society as you progress and mature in the financial world.

Chapter 15

The Final Four—Tips on Restructuring, Computers, Property Records, and Depositions

This book was never intended to be a "how to" on every possible accounting/financial hurdle along your career path. However, this section of the book, which deals with material that you probably didn't cover at great length in school, would be incomplete without a brief commentary on these four matters. Even if you are not confronted with these issues right away, a little more intimacy on the subjects may be of value to you.

Restructuring—Sometimes Painful, but Necessary

In *Random House Unabridged Dictionary* (second edition), restructure is defined as "to affect a fundamental change in (an organization or system)." This common word and simple definition was unheard of in financial jargon years ago. But pick up any copy of *The Wall Street Journal* over the last ten years, and you are almost sure to find an announcement about a company incurring a special restructuring charge. The amounts are usually staggering, and for some of the larger Fortune 500 companies, the charges have been in the billions. The basis for the charge can include every item in the spectrum of business activity—closing and relocating factories, making huge reductions in the employee workforce, writing off goodwill and intangibles, and disposing of unprofitable product lines and/or divisions. As you know under current accounting rules, the cost of the restructuring must be charged against current year income, and it often results in bringing the bottom line to a loss position. Nevertheless, the financial markets often perceive restructuring as a strong and positive move that augurs for improved profitability in the future. Accordingly, restructuring announcements are often followed by an increase in the company's share price on the public stock exchanges. It wasn't always like this. When I came into the business world, management, in general, was terribly reluctant to bite the bullet and take a big hit. The tendency was for companies to hold onto losers, and year-in and year-out tinker with ways to fix them—restructuring just wasn't the thing to do.

I was not able to learn the date and identity of the first company announcement of a restructuring, but I would venture a guess that it was one mandated by a financial crisis. As these restructurings began to receive approvals in the financial markets, their use proliferated even to very successful companies who viewed restructuring as an effective management tool that could be used for prudent financial housecleaning.

The concept of corporate restructuring may originate solely from the CEO and/or the board of directors, but more likely restructuring has its roots in a think-tank session of a corporate strategies planning meeting when all of the senior executives play the game of "what if." In today's financial world the number one objective of public companies is to enhance stockholder value. Because of intimate knowledge of the company's financial data, it is the CFO who has to carry the ball and pro forma restructuring ideas from his or her fellow officers and render an opinion on its feasibility and, of course, the expected improvement in stockholder value. If case histories of all restructurings were available I would bet that the concept for most of them originated with the CFO, simply because of his or her keen understanding of a company's financial structure and how various restructuring possibilities can affect the bottom line and stockholder value.

Once the board has approved a restructuring plan, it will fall upon the CFO to fine tune the numbers and orchestrate the plan. In this connection let me offer this advice: "Prepare a set of working papers that dot every 'i,' cross every 't,' and document every number in the plan."

There are two reasons for this extra care. The first is the matter of your important internal financial statements and the importance of keeping comparative financial data on an apples-to-apples basis. Good working papers will enable you to correctly restate prior-period financial data needed for current reports. Moreover, the working papers will enable you to reconcile your internal financial statements with those reported to shareholders, which must be prepared under special FASB. accounting rules. A second reason for the need of good working papers is to make your life easier when you are dealing with an IRS agent. The company will have recorded a huge restructuring change that undoubtedly includes anticipated future costs and expenses. Obviously, careful records must be maintained to support the proper deduction according to the current and/or appropriate taxable year.

Whether you are with a CPA firm or on a company's controller's staff, there's a very good chance that you'll be involved with a restructuring. If you are involved, remember this message of "good working papers."

The Forgotten Property Records

On your first day of Accounting 101 suppose the instructor went to the blackboard and wrote the following:

Assets (in thousands)	xyz Corp.
Cash	150
Accounts receivable	850
Property, plant, & equipment	1,800
Inventories	750
Prepared expenses	50
Total	$ 3,600

Then he turned to the class and said, "Companies keep different records for each of their asset categories. Looking at xyz's assets, which one do you suppose will have the best records?" I know what I would have said, and I bet that most of the class would also say, "Property, plant, and equipment." Is it like that in the real world? Absolutely not! Property record-keeping in industrial organizations is usually pretty sad—if there are records, they are not up to date, they don't agree with the general ledger, they can't be reconciled with appraisals made by professional organizations, and they don't reflect all of the adjustments made by IRS agents in prior tax audits. Based on my audit experience, public utilities, railroads, and big oil companies maintain good property records, but in total these industry groups constitute only a small percent of corporate America.

Failure to keep good property records is not a life-threatening matter to a successful industrial concern. There are, however, some decided pluses that make it worthwhile for the time and effort involved in establishing and maintaining good property records.

One absolute key to an effective property control system is a periodic physical inventory to verify that the respective tangible assets shown by the records are on hand and in the location where they are supposed to be. If the books and the physical inventory are reasonably in agreement—well and good. But if they are not, it may mean "trouble in River City." Theft, mysterious disappearance, unreported scrapping, equipment failures, equipment obsolescence, and maintenance difficulties loom as some of the possibilities that may account for differences between the books and the physical inventories. These are problems that a company can address quickly before they become rooted and significant. In the absence of a good system, a company could be unaware of such problems for an extended period, and when they finally come to the surface, the problems may be serious.

From the standpoint of the company CEO and board of directors, a good property system will provide the assurance that the company's property, plant, and equipment shown on the balance sheet is on hand and in good condition. From the standpoint of accounting and tax benefits, a good property system will enable the accounting department to do a more accurate job in its departmental depreciation and maintenance charges, and for tax purposes it will provide the correct depreciation expense and the required information for claiming deductions for early abandonments, scrapping, and obsolescent write-offs.

There is an enormous amount of data involved in a good property record system. I think that is the prime reason property records were neglected in the precomputing era. That is no longer the case today because excellent software programs are available. It may be a big job to put in a computerized property system, but once installed, it can function smoothly without a lot of time and effort.

When you have the opportunity, look over your client's and/or company's property accounting records. More than likely you'll find an area where you can someday roll up your sleeves on a special project that will pay handsome dividends to the client/company.

Don't Blame the Computer

My first look at computers was on the John Morrell & Company audit in 1948. The meat packing industry was one of the leaders in using the computer for more than just an accounting machine, and as a young rookie just out of college, I marveled at the incredible office and accounting tasks that those IBM machines could perform. Throughout my entire career I continued to marvel at each new generation of computers and how its uses and applications spread from the business office to space research, medicine, engineering, and other vital segments of our society. Our country's amazing achievements in the Gulf War, and the fact it lasted only forty-two days, were due to our skilled Armed Forces using arsenals of high tech weapons and military strategies developed with the aid of computers.

The computer has also been responsible for many incredible gains in our living standards, yet in our daily lives, it is much maligned and the frequent scapegoat for all kinds of petty mistakes and delays in the processing of data. I'm sure you've heard statements like, "We can't change your statement, sir, the computer won't let us," or "The computer is down, so we can't do anything about your problem. Call us next week."

Fortunately, in business, the computer is revered for what it is—one of the marvels of the ages. But nothing is perfect, and there will be an occasional equipment failure that can bring about brief periods of downtime. There can also be reports coming out of the data processing department that are absolutely crazy. The first inclination is to blame the computer, but that would be silly. We all should know that the computer is designed to obey every command to the letter. A number of years ago someone coined the phrase "garbage in – garbage out" as an explanation for fiascoes in computer reports and procedures. The phrase absolves the computer and puts the blame exactly where it belongs—on the backs of systems analysts and programmers who designed the procedures and the instructions for the input of the data and the processing thereof. This leads us to the point of the chapter. The data processing department should report directly to the chief accounting officer who should maintain effective control over all data processing programs and functions. It should be his or her responsibility to insure that the data and reports prepared by the data processing department are subject to accounting control and tie in with the general accounting records. The chief accounting officer must require appropriate audit trails and a system of checks and balances to insure that the reports coming out of the data processing department are realistic and reliable.

My experiences with data processing personnel led me to believe that they are a special breed. They are creative, dedicated, and hard working and understandably want the newest equipment the day after it is announced, and if they are not controlled, they tend to run wild. Their systems and programming activities should be carefully planned and monitored and their utilization of the department's expensive equipment and any proposed equipment replacement should always be subject to cost justification. If the data processing department does not report to the CFO or the chief accounting officer I would still strongly recommend that the controls I've spoken about are the responsibility of a senior officer, and that officer should work very closely with the chief accounting officer or the CFO on such matters.

The investment in equipment, software, and personnel make the data processing department one of the most expensive departments in most companies. Accordingly, state of the art department security, passwords, and access to the system, as well as emergency backup procedures and record storage are essential and important parts of the department's total operation. Owing to the continuing development of new equipment and software, as well as the rapid pace and changes of the department's activities, it is a logical candidate for a periodic (every couple of years) review by an outside professional organization to make certain the company is getting the full amount of benefits for every dollar spent.

In closing this chapter, I want to emphasize that the tie-in of data processing reports with general accounting is an absolute requirement in a system of effective financial control. I would also like to add a practical suggestion about the data processing department. They are called upon to issue all kinds of special reports. Generally, these reports will run forever, unless the department is notified to stop their preparation. It is therefore important that every year or two a complete survey should be made of all data processing reports. The survey should include interviews with the recipients to verify the usefulness and the continuing need for the report. Typically, this survey will kill off a lot of reports and free up invaluable computer time for newer and more important applications.

Depositions—Not a Picnic by Any Means

During my first sixty years on this planet my only contact with depositions was viewing Perry Mason whodunits on late night TV. Then suddenly, I am personally involved in a law suit in connection with my stock ownership in an insurance company, and my employer, Woodhead Industries, is involved in a proxy fight and is also sued as an outgrowth of two divestitures. In prosecuting these matters, I had to give depositions five or six times. They were very demanding experiences that I'll remember for a long time. The fact that I had that many depositions is pure chance—I just happened to be a bystander in an action between two parties. Chances are you'll never have to give a deposition in your career, but if you do, here are a few suggestions.

Your lawyer will prep you (sort of a dress rehearsal) before the deposition and give you a lot of useful advice. They'll tell you that the purpose of the deposition is to confirm or clarify a lot of evidence already known through the discovery process and also to find more evidence through the deposition process. More evidence is discovered when the person being deposed becomes too talkative and starts answering questions with unnecessary explanations to questions that can and should be answered with a simple yes or no. The lawyer will tell you to take your time, don't rush. He/She will tell you to answer "I don't know" if you're not sure, and they'll tell you to ask for clarification if you don't understand the question. You are under oath of course, and they'll remind you that you must be 100% truthful in your answers.

The reason for my telling you about this now is merely an affirmation from me (a veteran of six depositions) that the prepping and advice from your lawyer should be heeded and followed to the letter. I must confess that I took counsel's advice too lightly before my first deposition. Consequently, it was a terribly grueling experience because I was not mentally prepared. It's like anything you do for the first time—you just don't do it well. Remember also, that you are an amateur in this arena going one-on-one with a skillful professional lawyer with years of experience. Obviously, don't get cute and try and outsmart them because they'll catch you every time. Give the truth and nothing else and you'll have no problem; give something other than the truth and you'll regret it, because it will probably come back to haunt you.

Part III.

Forty Years in the Financial World–
Reflections and Experiences

Chapter 16

The World of the Big Six

The ink was barely dry on my diploma before I boarded the Rock Island Rocket for Chicago on a cold day in February, 1948. Two hours later I was in the Price Waterhouse office filling out the usual personnel forms for new employees and receiving my "busy season" assignments. I had received assurance earlier from the recruiter that they could probably accommodate my request for a lot of out-of-town work, particularly in the first year. The top starting salary of $200 per month in those days could barely support even the most Spartan kind of existence in Chicago, and by living off the expense account for awhile, I could avoid draining my limited cash resources. I was elated to receive my work schedule; good clients in Indianapolis, Racine, Wisconsin, and Cedar Rapids, Iowa. This would carry me through July. I was also given a cash advance for travel expenses, a first class ticket (including Pullman sleeper) leaving for Indianapolis that evening, and a confirmed reservation at the best hotel in the city. At six o'clock I was sitting in the train's club car reading the afternoon paper and sipping a Canadian Club and soda. I was on cloud nine but nervous about the next day. I didn't have the benefit of the firm's training class, held in September, and had no idea of what to expect when I joined the audit team. All I could do was give it my best shot. At any rate my career was launched, and little did I know that I would be in this world of debits and credits until my retirement from business forty years later.

Back in 1948, the Big Eight now the Big Six, was virtually unknown to the general public. Rumor has it that the average man on the street thought the Big Six was some kind of athletic conference. Here are the original Eight which you may recognize despite a few name changes and mergers.

1) Arthur Andersen
2) Arthur Young

3) Ernst & Ernst
4) Haskins and Sells
5) Lybrand Ross Bros. & Montgomery
6) Peat Marwick and Mitchell
7) Price Waterhouse
8) Touche Nevin Bailey and Smart

The practice of public accounting was a relatively new business in the United States, having its origin in the early 1900s as an outgrowth and expansion of chartered accounting firms in Great Britain. Price Waterhouse was a typical example. It was formed in England in 1860 by S.H. Price and Eloisus Waterhouse and grew in concert with the rapid industrialization in the latter part of the nineteenth century. As British companies formed subsidiary companies in America, Price Waterhouse opened offices to take care of their needs, and when American industrialization got into high gear a little bit later, these experienced British firms were on hand to take care of their accounting needs. From this beginning, the growth of accounting firms was favorably augmented from time to time by government legislation such as:

1913 - Federal Reserve Act
1914 - Federal Trade Commission
1916 - Federal Income Taxes
1933 - Securities Act

The enactment of the 1933 Securities Act was the most significant. It was an attempt to remedy the ills of the securities business that surfaced during the 1929 stock market crash. But it was soon apparent that the legislation did not go far enough, and as a result Congress created the SEC in June 1934. (With tongue in cheek it has been called the greatest Accountant's Employment Act ever.) Among the provisions of the law:

> "All securities listed on the various exchanges would be registered with the SEC and the companies issuing them would have to publish annual reports prepared by independent accountants."

This legislation also required that any new securities could not be issued to the public unless they were first registered with the SEC. Such registration was to include financial statements prepared by independent accountants. In the words of humorist Will Rogers, the government had finally "put a cop on Wall Street."

The impact of the SEC requirements triggered the enormous growth of CPA firms. As the general public, private businesses, and lending institutions became more familiar with these firms and the value of certified financial statements, they became significant clients of CPA organizations. When I joined the Chicago office of Price Waterhouse in 1948, there were approximately 100 professionals on the staff—today there are over 1,000. Worldwide, Price Waterhouse has about 50,000 professionals, an employment level matched by other Big Six firms.

Worldwide revenues in 1994 for each of the Big Six firms were in a range of five to seven billion dollars—a figure that would have been considered unthinkable forty years ago. Although I left Price Waterhouse in 1955, I never left the world of the Big Six. Throughout the rest of my career I dealt with a Big Six firm at the end of each fiscal year and many times throughout the year in connection with merger and acquisition investigations, audit committee meetings, or Federal Income Tax matters.

One month after I retired in May of 1988 my son John joined Arthur Andersen as a manager on the audit staff. Through him, I still feel connected to the world of the Big Six and am able to watch it continue to grow and develop. It is interesting to see how Big Six firms have changed so much and yet there are many facets of life in the Big Six that show little change from my time.

Then and Now—Things are Not What They Used to Be.

Salaries and Benefits
Earlier I mentioned that the top starting salary in the Big Six in 1948 was $200 per month. At the time, top students were starting at $300 per month in Fortune 500 companies. The disparity can be explained by the fact that most Big Six firms had their roots as chartered accountants in England, where beginning employees (who were called articles) worked without pay for a year or two as part of their education. This was undoubtedly the force behind a very chintzy salary scale during the first few years with the Big Six firms. Gradually, this old salary philosophy faded away, and with the public accountant's emergence as a highly respected professional, beginning salaries of $30,000 plus are for the most part the top salaries attainable for graduating accounting seniors joining Big Six organizations. The same holds true for all the perks—insurance, overtime, vacations—are all drastically better than in the so called good old days.

Continuing Education

In my seven years at Price Waterhouse, I can't recall ever attending seminars or training classes on new accounting issues. I think the reason is that there simply wasn't much happening in the financial world in those years that would cause changes in financial statements and audit procedures that would warrant the need for special classes.

LIFO inventory was starting to appeal to more companies, and the Korean War resulted in an excess profits tax in 1951. But other than isolated items like this, audits were sort of a repetitive ho-hum during this period. By contrast, the audits of the nineties are bulging with very demanding new issues resulting from requirements under FASB (Financial Accounting Standards Board) and the SEC. To keep abreast of these matters and the new rules coming out each year, be prepared to attend seminars as well as annual training classes now held by all leading accounting firms. As a matter of fact, a program of continuing education is now required for holders of a CPA certificate, a practical approach that was long overdue. To some extent, this will also assure a continuing program of self-development for practicing CPAs.

Audit Fee Management

The combination of a relatively lower salary scale and less complicated and time consuming audits were factors that alleviated client pressure to hold down audit fees years ago. That is not the case today. The high salary levels coupled with the many new audit requirements imposed by FASB & SEC rules have resulted in the difficult challenge for accounting firms of managing the audit so as to achieve optimum results for all chargeable hours. Planning the audit is now a much more important function, and establishing chargeable time goals and obtaining approval of the audit scope and approximate audit fee from the client's audit committee are very essential parts of the audit plan. With billing rates in a range of $100 to $400 dollars per hour, a long workday, even by beginning junior auditors, will amount to over $1,000 of audit fees. It is therefore paramount that hours on the job are totally productive and free of gossip sessions and long lunches. It is not surprising then, that in large audits, a member of the client's controller's staff will keep tabs on the auditors while they are on the job.

Consulting Systems and Other Management Services

The amount of systems and management consulting work done by the Chicago office of Price Waterhouse in 1948 was so little, you could put it in a thimble. As a matter of fact, I recall that the total systems department was one employee, a good professional and a nice guy who took quite a razzing because his name was Harold Price (no relation to the firm's founder). Today their Price Waterhouse Chicago office has over five hundred professionals outside of the audit staff. In addition to systems and management consulting, they do tax planning, valuations, strategic planning, and a host of other consulting assignments on matters such as insurance and financing. The number of professionals in these activities is now greater than the audit staff and confirms the many opportunities besides auditing in a Big Six organization. Starting as a junior auditor may be the initial stepping stone to a future position as a partner in management consulting.

CPAs' Opinions and Work Scope

The standard opinion or certificate used when I joined Price Waterhouse in 1948 did not change one iota until recently when a long overdue change was finally made. The new opinion more clearly sets forth what the audit scope is all about and management's involvement in the financial statements. These changes in the language of the opinion has not altered in any way the work done in a current examination of a company's financial statements. Cash, receivables, and payables continue to be confirmed or verified by other means, physical inventories are observed, and securities are counted, as has been done by independent auditors for decades. What has happened, however, is a substantial amount of new work is now required under the many pronouncements by the FASB, and there is greater emphasis on internal controls and cash flow. In addition, the global expansion of so many American companies has added the complexities of foreign exchange and many other challenging accounting issues that were not prevalent years ago.

Then and Now - Some Things Never Change

Personal Appearance and Demeanor

There were virtually no women on audit staffs in the late 1940s, and so there were no dress codes for them. The dress code for male staff members, however, was very explicit—conservative suits and white shirts and ties at all times, except weekend work when the clients' offices were closed. It was rigidly enforced, and any male staff member reporting for work in sport coats and loud apparel combinations would receive *one* gentle reminder. If he didn't go along with the suggestions, it was "goodbye." Some forty years later this continues to be the same dress code the Big Six firms follow today. The matters of dress codes for men and women, appearance, and demeanor are covered in detail in Part I, Chapter 3.

On-the-Job Training for Another Job

I don't remember anyone in my starting class at Price Waterhouse who was aiming at a career with the firm. Rather, they were trying to get sufficient experience to (1) land a good job in industry in the accounting/financial departments or in management, or (2) learn the CPA business well enough to establish their own practice or join a smaller firm as a partner. One of my classmates, John Biegler, was an exception. He was an engineering major in college, but fell in love with his work at Price Waterhouse and went on to become the senior partner of the U.S. firm in the sixties and seventies. From my discussions and observations of graduating accounting majors, the using of Big Six experience as a faster stepping stone to senior accounting positions continues to be the primary reason for seeking employment with a Big Six firm. In this connection, I want to make a suggestion that may be of significant value later in your career. It is something that I did not do but wish I had, and it doesn't take a lot of time. Buy a business diary and make brief entries after the conclusion of each audit assignment. In a few years you will have a library of accurate and valuable information that you wouldn't have just by trusting your experiences to memory. Let me give you an example of a possible entry.

> *July 15 to Aug 8, 1994, LSK Food Co.*
> Worked on cash—company had efficient book and cash procedures to speedup collections—worked on product costs, records were terrible—industrial engineer's data never tied in with the books. Company's earnings are flat and going no place. Marketing head is a dork—J.P. Doe controller is a sharp guy. Phone # (234) 456-7000.

These crib notes would be sufficient for you to more easily recall the details behind these matters that you might use when you encounter similar situations at other clients, or related problems later in your career. If you had a good rapport with client personnel, what could be better than a phone call to an old business friend for your needed information or assistance.

Working Papers

My audit course at the University of Illinois covered all of the usual audit theory and included a rather outdated audit problem that stretched out for the entire semester. There was virtually no focus on the importance and preparation of good working papers. On my very first audit assignment in Indianapolis, I would have been a "lost duck" if it hadn't been for good working papers from the prior year's audit. They provided an outline on how to go about doing the work for the current year's audit. The importance of good and complete working papers was a requirement that had to be fulfilled even though the accounts had been settled with the client and the audit itself was signed off. This continues to be a hallmark of CPA firms, and I don't believe it is stressed enough in the classroom. Your performance ratings on audit assignments will be enhanced by your preparations of neat and thorough working papers.

Integrity

As you may know, in order to be truly independent, CPA firms have a number of rules. One such rule is not to have a personal stock investment in a client. In addition, all firms have a laundry list of do's and don'ts covering expense account procedures, on the job conduct, etc. Throughout all of these rules, there is an overriding, implied demand of professional integrity at all times. It means total honesty in the preparation of working papers and in your verification of audit programs and work done. It is very easy to fudge and not check *every* page of inventory as may be required by the program, or to sign the payables program for having inspected all supporting documents when you only checked half of them, or showing on your time sheet that you worked six hours on a Sunday when you only worked two hours. In any large organization there are probably a few employees who will bend the rules, cheat, or whatever. They are, however, their own worst enemy. First, if they are ever caught, and that is quite likely, they will be fired outright and can never receive a good reference evaluation from the CPA firm. Secondly, if they are not caught by the CPA firm, they will probably continue to cheat, and later in their career will be caught cheating on another job. The need for integrity and fidelity in business is timeless. It always was and always will be.

The Client Comes First

One comment I never heard said to a client was, "we'll start the audit a week late because the in-charge senior is on vacation." Quite obviously, big CPA firms could not exist without satisfied clients who pay very substantial fees for their services. The client's responsibility is to operate a profitable business for its shareholders, and in doing so will schedule its accounting closings, audits, and physical inventories according to what is best for the company. This may result in a lot of untimely work for the auditor—inventories on New Year's Eve, evening and weekend work, or travel over busy holiday periods. The rapport with most clients is top-notch, and they will do their best to cooperate with their auditors. But remember when something ends in a tie the client comes first.

There is a little more to this matter of "client first;" it is what I call client loyalty. It shows up in the little things that auditors do, that over time add up to lasting goodwill. It is certain that a good auditor will come across practices and procedures during the course of the audit that could be improved or simplified. They may not be so major as to warrant inclusion in a formal procedure memorandum, but they can be practical ideas for the client's accounting staff. Showing how a "proof of cash" can help in checking bank reconciliation and setting up income tax working papers so that they tie in with the general ledger, are examples of the hundreds of helpful tips that a client might welcome. To hear some smart-alec auditor charge into the controller's office and make a big deal out of an arithmetic error found in the balance of the unexpired insurance account is not a welcome tip. This may happen sometimes because young auditors seem to have a preconceived notion that they must find mistakes, so when they do, they are apt to get carried away. Whether it is a small matter or a major issue, the magic word for an auditor to remember is "finesse"—get your point across constructively but with professional class.

The above sections dealing with growth, changes, and the general environment of the Big Six over the last forty years hopefully will give you an overall practical feel for the accounting business and what you might expect as an employee. It's an exciting field, but tough and competitive. It's also a marvelous way to get a quick and accurate insight into the financial world. Most likely your experience will be different than mine, but some of my experiences may have learning value that are not affected by time. Here are some that you might find interesting.

Defalcations

Audits are not designed to detect defalcations, but recent pressures by Congress and the SEC may require changes in this area. Case studies show that defalcations are usually perpetrated and carried out by smart employees who know the systems, and therefore, can design a slick method for absconding with company assets. But like the perfect crime, they are more often caught or detected purely by accident. Here are examples of two such schemes.

Case History #1 - The Purchasing Agent
   During the usual discussions with management at the onset of an annual audit, we were informed by the general manager of a large machinery manufacturer about the rich lifestyle of the division purchasing agent. He was paid a moderate salary and had no apparent source of other income, yet he owned a beautiful house, belonged to the area's best clubs, drove a new Cadillac, and travelled to only the best places on vacations and holidays. Management considered him to be a top purchasing agent and never observed anything in his work that would suggest any irregularity or impropriety. Nevertheless, management felt that we should know about this "just in case." As the audit proceeded, it was noted that the salary checks issued to the suspicious purchasing agent were deposited in a small bank in a remote city many miles away. By itself, it was nothing to be alarmed about, but later in the audit during a routine counting of the petty cash, we found checks in the petty cash fund drawn by the purchasing agent on a local bank. The cashier told us that the suspected individual frequently cashed personal checks for the $100 maximum allowed under company policy. This, of course, was pretty strong evidence that he did have some other source of income, and this was reported to the general manager. He suggested that we conduct some detailed checking into the purchasing department. To do this more effectively without arousing suspicion, he sent the purchasing agent out of town for a week to attend an industry trade show. We literally tore the agent's department records apart, and in a few days his clever scheme was unveiled. The agent had set up a dummy corporation with the help of a relative in a remote city where he deposited his company payroll check. From time to time, the purchasing agent would issue a purchase order to the dummy corporation for technical machinery and/or supplies for which the price was not really known or publicized and not readily available to anyone except the purchasing agent. The dummy corporation would then issue a purchase order to an established company with instructions to drop-ship the order to the purchasing agent's factory. The dummy corporation in turn would bill the purchasing agent's company at twice the price

charged to the dummy corporation by the established manufacturer. The dummy corporation's invoice would be approved by the purchasing agent, and along with the receiving report, would be sent to the treasurer's department for payment in the usual course of business. This scheme had been in play for three or four years at the rate of about $75,000 per year. The purchasing agent was very astute; he reported these stolen funds on his income tax returns and also invested the money successfully in real estate. When he was caught, he had funds available to return the stolen money to the company. Ironically, he engaged Price Waterhouse to prepare federal income refund claims for the absconded funds previously reported as income on his personal return.

Case History #2 - The Secretary of the Board

The client was a medium-sized private University located in the Midwest. University and/or college audits are somewhat complex. In addition to dealing with some of the unusual aspects of fund accounting, the school operations include many businesses under one roof—restaurants, gift shops, housing, athletic departments, entertainment centers, to name some of the more important ones. Although the bulk of the school's revenues was from tuition, the income from endowment funds, restricted gifts, and other sources was significant. The audit had proceeded routinely except for one major problem. The secretary of the board had left for a long summer vacation. He was also the business manager who ran the endowment funds and all financial matters. He had held this post for a number of years, was a real intellectual, but a little sloppy on details and audit trails. Consequently, explanations for certain entries were not always available from files or backup materials. The answers were in the secretary's head. The problem was compounded further because the controller, though very capable, was a newcomer and of little help on prior matters. Nevertheless the audit proceeded in all phases except for a few accounts in the Endowment Fund related to the University's substantial investment in home real estate mortgages. These activities were administered solely by the secretary of the board with token assistance by a clerk in his office. Their accounting for new real estate mortgage loans was a little tricky. Funds were transferred from a general bank account to a special "loan bank account" that was used to record all disbursements made on behalf of the borrower's loan. After the real estate closing, any differences were settled with the borrower and transferred to "Miscellaneous Endowment Receivables." Even though the control balance in this account was less than $100, I examined it anyway. I have always believed that an auditor must know how every account works no matter how immaterial it appears to be. I remember scanning the subsidiary ledger and being surprised at the number of open balances. Because of the secretary's absence, I decided to make a test of the account. I made a few random selections which disclosed that many open credit balances were being settled by check with the borrower many months after the loan had been taken out and apparently fully processed. Moreover, these settlements came in bunches—maybe ten or twenty at a time.

It didn't make sense to me. I became even more curious as I examined all the cancelled checks related to the mortgages I had randomly selected. The endorsements on the final settlement check to the borrower all had a strange similarity. They were all cashed locally that same day (almost an impossibility since some of the borrowers lived in neighboring suburbs). A more careful review of the endorsement disclosed that they were all forged—having been traced from the borrowers signature on the loan application. We confirmed this with the borrower and knew for certain that we had a defalcation on our hands. It seems that the secretary became disgruntled over a less than expected salary increase and almost immediately started the scheme with the real estate mortgages. When he saw how easy it was, he went after funds in other ways—writing off accounts and then personally collecting the amount, skimming cash receipts from University functions, etc. We discovered the latter when we expanded the audit work to include a detailed review of all transactions under his control, direct and indirect.

When we finished, the total defalcation was over $50,000, a considerable sum in the early fifties. The matter came to an end when we scheduled a meeting with the secretary in a downtown hotel suite in order to report our findings and give him an opportunity to challenge or deny them. We went through our list one at a time. There were so many small items it took over an hour to complete the task. He readily admitted every transaction, and when we asked him why he did it, he put his head in his hands and said "Only the Master knows." Then he quickly moved his right hand into his inside coat pocket. In a flash I visualized a colt revolver blazing away at me, and it would be curtains for yours truly. I guess that only happens in today's TV specials, because the repentant secretary pulled out a handkerchief and wiped his tearful eyes. The secretary was very prominent in civic affairs, and because the defalcations involved so many people, the whole town soon knew about it. Accordingly the district attorney felt compelled to indict him even though all the funds were returned.

That was the only time in my life I ever appeared before a grand jury, an experience I'm happy I never had to repeat. He pleaded guilty and received a light sentence in a white-collar prison.

This second example shows the most extreme reverberation of what might happen when you look over all the records in an audit and see how even these tiny general ledger accounts work. The moral of the story: All small balances are not always unimportant and immaterial.

Fifty-Strong March on the Bank

The point of this story is to illustrate that Big Six accounting firms become involved in a variety of one-time special audits and/or reviews, and no matter how unusual, the firms have the brainpower and manpower to get the job done.

Except for a handful of major banks whose stocks were held by the public, most banks in the early fifties relied on the statutory examinations of its records made by bank examiners. So it was somewhat of a surprise when a principal bank in a medium-sized Midwestern city engaged Price Waterhouse for a full-blown balance sheet audit—it was to be done on the occasion of the bank's 75th anniversary. The preparations and planning for this audit were certainly unusual. First of all, there were no prior years' working papers to use as guides, and secondly, there was virtually no bank auditing experience among the personnel in the Chicago office. After several meetings with the bank's CEO, the audit details were worked out.

Fifty auditors would be required to take over and control bank operations for about two working days—the estimated interval to clear and account for all bank assets. The bank's premises and work stations were diagramed on a large drawing and in a "war room" the team of fifty auditors learned their specific assignments. The audit was to start at exactly 3:00 PM, shortly before regular closing time. At that time the fifty auditors would enter the bank premises, the CEO would announce the beginning of the audit over the public address system, the auditors would pin identification badges on their lapels, and the audit would be under way. As a protective measure, the travel arrangements for the fifty auditors were staggered and varied (some by car, some by train, etc.) so they would not arouse a lot of curiosity in the central business district. Of course, the chief of police was notified early that day so as to eliminate any possible police reaction to fifty well-dressed men descending on the bank from all directions at the same time.

The audit was short but quite interesting. Since we had no prior experience with the bank, it was guesswork as to what the problems might be and the manpower needed at the various work stations (teller cages, collateral cages, etc.) It was a play it by ear situation with everybody pitching in where needed. I was in charge of the work in the trust department, and we were able to establish the controls and necessary verifications by 10:00 that evening. However, the work was proceeding at a much slower pace in other bank areas, because most of the bank's record keeping was done manually. I helped out in the vault, assisting with counting the reserve cash which totaled over a million dollars in mostly small bills. Shortly after 1:00 AM we had accomplished our first day's mission of establishing the controls and the related verifications at the different teller cages and work stations. In another day or two the bank audit was complete except for the review of procedures and controls. I was in charge of the separate audit of the trust department and found it to be the most interesting part of the bank's total operations. The trust department was involved in a variety of interesting investment and management assignments, as well as the administration of wills, court appointments, etc. Otherwise, the principle banking business as I saw it then was pretty routine, and the top jobs seemed perfunctory and without challenge. Since that time, banks have become more creative and aggressive, and undoubtedly there now exists improved opportunities for qualified accounting professionals.

Professionalism at Work

The relationships between the big CPA firms and their clients is usually very cordial. After all, doing an audit year-in and year-out, the people involved are certain to become very well-acquainted, and it's almost inevitable that friendships will develop. If it is a business friendship, it makes for top-notch cooperation and more efficient and lower cost audits. However, if the relationship is replete with socializing and entertainment throughout the year, and grows into a buddy-buddy situation, the auditor may find themselves in a danger zone where close personal friendship and a profitable audit fee may take away from their independence when confronted with some sticky issues on the audit. Will the auditor remember that their opinion, although addressed to their client, is issued to the world—the company's stockholders, employees, investment bankers, customers, suppliers, etc.?

During my years at Price Waterhouse, I found that a very cordial relationship existed with all of the clients, but we had to be careful about the amount of socializing. An annual golf outing, baseball game, theater, or dinner was okay in order to stay in touch, but must be done in moderation throughout the year. I really didn't appreciate the importance of being absolutely independent until we ran into a stalemate with a prestigious and friendly client about disclosing the fair market value of an obscure investment, with a small cost basis that had mushroomed into a huge market value. The client did not want to disclose this, fearing it might attract too much takeover interest. The client anticipated that the auditors would raise the disclosure question, and accordingly developed a very thin rationale in support of their position. I remember reviewing this entire matter with the senior partner at breakfast before driving to the client's office to settle the accounts. His response was along these lines: "I would hate to lose this fine NYSE company as a client after all these years, but we must disclose the market value. If we lose the client, Price Waterhouse can survive and we will not have lost our independence." The senior partner was invited to the board meeting that morning when the troublesome issue was to be discussed. When the board meeting was over, a smiling chairman exited the room with an arm around the senior partner—the market value of that investment was disclosed, and that company is still a client today. (I never did ask how he handled the board, but he obviously convinced them that disclosure was the firm's best and only course.)

Back in the 1950s it was relatively easy to change auditors. Today that isn't the case because the SEC wants to know why. Nevertheless, the principle of independence by the CPA firms is just as important today as it was in the fifties. It is an ever present and overriding discipline that the auditor must never forget, even if it results in losing a client from time to time. In the long run the auditor will be better off.

Physical Inventory Observations

Earlier in this book, there was an entire chapter, "Taking Care of Inventories," that dealt with many facets of physical inventory, an important asset on most company balance sheets. Despite its dollar significance, the taking of physical inventory is one category where companies tend to be lax and sloppy. Consider this: most companies take only one physical inventory a year, so they certainly are not steeped in experience even though some of the inventory crew may have worked on earlier physicals. However, since physical inventories are taken at the "wrong times" (weekends, New Years, and other holidays) the bulk of the work is assigned to the newer employees with the least seniority and physical inventory experience. Now add another negative to the situation—plant employees are just not good with simple arithmetic. They can count a simple stack of boxes, but when they start multiplying that count by the depth and length of a pile, enormous mistakes can and do happen. I have always wondered why the typical physical inventory is observed only by plant personnel and rarely top members of the company's financial and accounting departments. Their presence would tend to keep the employees on the ball.

For these reasons, you would think that the physical inventory work done by the CPA firms would be done by more experienced personnel. In my experience, that hasn't been the case. The observations are assigned to the lower ranking staff members. On the large inventory of an important client a manager may make an appearance, but I never saw a partner on any inventory observation. As a rookie you can expect to receive frequent physical inventory assignments, but despite your experience, you can do a bang-up job if you do the following.

1) Carefully study the inventory working papers and the physical inventory memorandum of the prior year's working papers. This will help you in focusing on the higher value items or any slow moving stock.

2) Try to obtain a copy of the company's inventory instructions before hand. If that cannot be done, obtain a copy as soon as you arrive at the company's plant, and review it with the employee in charge.

3) Do all the cutoff work first, paying particular attention to any physical activity or movement in the shipping and receiving area.

4) Tour the entire plant area and get a feel for the layout and product locations. Also get acquainted with the different count teams and discuss their programs.

5) Make your test counts with emphasis on the major items but try to make counting observations of every team if possible.

The above list of suggestions may well be included in the instructions you receive from your supervisors. They are very important, and so I've included them at the expense of being redundant.

One final comment on inventory observations: obviously, they are all a little different, but expect to run into the unexpected. Here are some that I ran into.

"We Saw No Critters"

The client was one of the world's leading oil companies, and I was lucky to be included on the staff assigned to do the annual audit. Their entire accounting system, internal controls, and financial reporting formats were state of the art. Every phase of the company's business was subject to the right checks and balances, and all entries in the general records were backed up with proper documentation. From my perspective, it was the ultimate benchmark which I frequently referred to in doing audits of other companies. Working on that audit for several year-ends was like doing advanced study toward a master's degree. It was not a surprise, therefore, when I was sent to the desolate plains of Oklahoma to check the inventories of crude oil stored in huge drums on oil tank farms. On inventory day, I picked up a Hertz rental car in the wee hours of the morning and headed for the first inventory site. I met the company representative at the appointed place—a small diner near the first tank farm. He was a veteran oil man and was dressed to fit the part—hard hat, boots, thick blue jeans, and a leather jacket. He was driving a heavy pickup truck, and he suggested we use his vehicle because the terrain around the oil tanks was a little rugged. That was an understatement—the dense growth of wild brush was knee high. Moreover, each storage tank was engulfed by a moat-like barrier—a mound of earth about three feet high, distanced about 60-80 feet from the outer edge of these enormous tanks. For fire protective measures the tanks were about 150-300 feet apart, and for each tank measurement we drove to the edge of the barrier, got out of the truck, waded through the brush to the tank, climbed the ladder to the top of the tank, checked the quantity as indicated by the perpetual stock ledger, and returned to the truck. (My CPA certificate wasn't needed for this job but strong legs were.) This ritual was repeated until late afternoon when we checked the last tank and then headed back to the diner for a cold beer.

As we enjoyed our drinks and chatted about the day, my host said that he was surprised "we saw no critters." "What do you mean by critters?" I asked. "Rattle snakes," he roared. "This is the rattlesnake capital of the world. Every year we have a hunt, and this year more than two thousand were captured over the weekends's festival." For a couple of seconds I was frozen with terror as my mind flashed back many years to the time when on a Boy Scout hike a big rattler made a strike at me and missed by inches. Had I known earlier that I was walking through rattlesnakes all day long, I don't know if I could have made it. We had another beer, and we talked a lot about snakes—I didn't leave Oklahoma with a sudden affection for rattlers, but I think I left that bar with less fear about those "critters."

What Happened to the Manager's Production?

The client was a prominent manufacturer and marketer of women's clothing with a number of factories, each specializing in making various kinds of garments for women. When I got the assignment to observe the physical inventory, I didn't react with a typical "oh no." The client was not terribly far from Chicago (I could drive it in about 2½ hours) and it was close to another city where following the inventory I could have a reunion and a golf game with one of my best friends from my old hometown. The working papers indicated that the inventory observation was very routine—and would have no problems. I drove to the client's office and arrived late in the afternoon at the appointed time. Preceding the taking of the physical inventory on the following day, I met the general manager and learned the bad news. Business was so good, and filling sales orders was so far behind schedule, that for the first time, factory production would not be stopped for the taking of the plant's annual physical inventory. Some creative physical inventory procedures had to be invented right then and there. The factory was about six stories high with all the bolts of woolens and other materials stored on the top floor. As production orders were processed, woolens and other raw materials were given a first cut and then moved to the fifth floor, fourth floor, etc., and depending on the style, could reach the first floor ready for shipment by the end of the workday. Women's suits required a good deal of handwork, button holes, etc., and the production of these garments was in process for several days. The skirts and the style in the early fifties required only a few cutting and sewing operations, and it was not any kind of production miracle to cut the materials in the morning and ship out a finished skirt before the five o'clock whistle.

The general manager was an experienced professional and with he and his key staff members, we worked out an elaborate scheme of in-plant cutoffs and documents to control all movement of materials and production as it flowed through the plant, and in some instances into trucks headed for customer's warehouses. The following morning every foreman spoke to his department employees about the importance of this physical inventory and the necessity that everyone cooperate and do whatever special assignment may be required. It was a wild day and my legs got a real workout up and down those six flights of stairs (there was an elevator, but typically it moved at a snail's pace when it was available). At the end of the day we were able to sort out the inventory according to raw materials, work in process, and finished goods, by reference to our special documents that accompanied all material and product movement in the plant that day. It was then that I observed that I had counted these as skirts in pieces at nine o'clock, and right now they were on their way to a Chicago customer." My assignment was completed satisfactorily, but the methodology was brand new compared to prior years. It is just another example that you should be prepared for the unexpected once in awhile when you observe physical inventories. No two inventories are alike, and they are not always the same as the last year.

Count the Legs and Divide by Four

I was packing up the working papers and getting ready to head for the train station and return to Chicago. It was a Friday and I was looking forward to watching the Fighting Illini play a football game on Saturday. The phone rang, and it was the office. The staff member assigned to observe the inventories at John Morrell's Topeka plant was ill, and I was the nearest and most available. I was given transportation instructions to get me there for the start of inventory on Saturday morning. The manager also assured me that the working papers would be there, and he filled me in on what to do. He said that the company had thousands of lambs in its feed lot and to be sure to check that carefully. This manager had a dry sense of humor and indicated that since I came from central-Illinois farm country, I should have no trouble with it. "But if you do," he said, "count the legs and divide by four."

The transportation arrangements were worked out, and I was on time for the Saturday inventories. While this was a year-end inventory, it was relatively easy because the company took material product and livestock inventories every month. The employees were really pros at this, and all of the inventories in the plant were finished by noon. After lunch, company employees took me to the feed lots for the livestock inventories. The company had detailed inventory records by pen, and it was a simple inventory instead of the nightmare I had expected. I was able to count one pen and multiply the count by the total number of pens to arrive at the total livestock number. (The stock records showed all pens to have the same number, and after counting one pen and verifying the quantity it was only a matter of looking over every pen and verify the reasonableness of the stock record quantity.) Because of this inventory observation and some other year-end work, I soon learned that my busy season schedule was changed to include the Topeka plant audit of John Morrell & Company. In time, Morrell became one of my biggest clients, and later my first position as an accounting officer in industry.

Hurray for the Bull Pen

The Price Waterhouse office in Chicago was located in three floors of the American National Bank Building on LaSalle Street. The partners and conference rooms occupied the top floor and were spacious and handsomely appointed. Conservatively, 95% of the firm's decorating budget must have been spent there, because the offices on the two lower floors were tiny, sterile, colorless cubicles that looked more like interrogating rooms in the New York Police precinct. The library was no exception—no pictures, no color, and most of the four gray walls were covered with black metal book cases filled with a good selection of accounting books, publications, and tax manuals. This cheerful place is where the rookies were required to be when they were unassigned between jobs. While in the library, unassigned personnel were supposed to spend all of their time reading accounting and tax material until called by the personnel manager for an assignment. The way the personnel manager went about this—opening the door and barking the name—was like a baseball manager calling the bull pen for a relief pitcher. It was only logical that the group started calling the library room the "bull pen"—a nickname that is still used there today.

I was only in the bull pen twice during my first year and each time for just a day or two. On one of these occasions I sat a long time next to a staff member who appeared to be studying a large tax manual. After a time I noticed, however, that this big manual was wrapped around a book. He was reading *The Nine Bad Shots of Golf*. I razzed him about this and jokingly told him I was going to report him. We had a good laugh and went to lunch together that day. I had played golf only a few times in my life and enjoyed it but could take it or leave it. However, at lunch I learned that the firm would give you the day off if you played in the annual Illinois CPA Golf Outing held at Medinah Country Club, one of the greatest courses in the world. (Three U.S. Opens have been held there and many other top golf tournaments.) My friend was reading the book to learn how to cure his slice and improve his game for the CPA Tournament. He gave me the book to browse over for a few days, and I found it fascinating. I couldn't wait for the weekend to try out the proper swing outlined in the text. That was the weekend that commenced my lifelong love affair with the game. In so many ways it shaped the course of my life for the better, both in my social life and in my business life. Today, as golf continues to grow in popularity and use in business situations, a single digit handicap is a very valuable skill to have in your arsenal of personal assets. Even if you have only average athletic skills, I believe it is worth your time and effort to develop a decent golf game for the business outings that are sure to come along.

The Plant Tour

Some lessons learned are never forgotten. They say riding a bicycle is one. In auditing I learned one in the early fifties from Bill Templeton, my favorite mentor at Price Waterhouse. On one of my earliest assignments as the senior-in-charge, Bill advised me, "Lloyd, when you get to the client's office, don't start immediately into the ledgers. After the usual few minutes of chitchat try to have a plant tour. You'll be amazed at how much you can learn from this. It will help you immensely in understanding the records throughout the audit. Pay attention to the inventories because if there are problems, you can expect to find them there."

Since that time, I never looked at a set of records without first looking over the operations. Believe me, it can tell you a lot about a company. As an example, let's take an imaginary tour of a typical manufacturing plant. Your tour guide will probably start by showing you the plant offices, such as industrial engineering, timekeeping, and material control. In each of these departments you will perhaps be introduced to the department head, and they will give you a minute or two run down on how the department operates. If the department head doesn't volunteer anything, don't be afraid to ask a polite question or two. Most department heads welcome the chance to talk to the auditors about their job and areas of responsibilities. The next part of the tour will take you to the factory, and more than likely to the receiving department where you will have an opportunity to see the incoming materials—finished parts and subassemblies that go directly to a furnished store's inventory bin, and raw material such as wire, sheet metal, etc., that go into raw material stores before going into production. While in the receiving area, see if you spot a lot of returned merchandise. This could be an obvious tip-off of product and warranty problems. If you observe this, don't be afraid to talk to the receiving department manager about it. They'll more than likely give you a lot of helpful information about the returned goods and warranty problems. Continuing on the tour, your guide will probably follow the flow of material throughout the factory as it passes through various machining processes into a finished parts storage bin and then onto the final assembly line and the finished goods inventory warehouse. As you follow the flow of product, you have a chance to observe the record keeping controls (if any) as product moves throughout the factory, and when it goes in and out of storerooms. This should give you a good perspective of the adequacy of the physical controls. As you inspect the various locations where inventories are stored, look carefully to see if the company maintains minimum quantity levels. Also, look for clues of dormant and inactive items and obvious overstocking. Many times you can find telltale evidence such as tags from previous inventories and the quantities on the tags indicating no usage for a couple of years. At all times on the tour, be observant of the pace, the cheerfulness, and alertness of the plant employees. You'll normally see these characteristics along with a hustle and bustle activity level in a good efficient factory operation. You will also notice good housekeeping in all departments (including the restrooms) of a top-notch factory operation. You can't prove cause and effect, but there is a distinct correlation—good factory housekeeping and good net income go together. Finally, make certain that you observe the procedures on the loading dock. One of the most critical points in a company's system of internal controls is assurance that all product that leaves the plant is billed. Our imaginary plant tour took less than two hours, and I can assure you it is probably the most productive two hours you can spend on an audit or a due diligence acquisition review.

At the Crossroads

The busy season (January to April) of 1955 was in full bloom when suddenly and quite unexpectedly, I was faced with the proverbial $64 watershed decision—do I stay with Price Waterhouse and make public accounting my career, or do I take an alternative position with one of my favorite clients? Price Waterhouse decided to open an office in a city where I had done most of all the audit work for the past three or four years and the senior partner offered me the opportunity to be in charge of that office.

This opportunity virtually assured me the chance of becoming a partner in a relatively short time. This was very appealing to me. It was financially attractive, a prestigious position, and the work was both challenging and satisfying. I was confident and comfortable in my work at Price Waterhouse. I knew my work well, and the clients liked me. On the negative side, however, I sometimes felt let down after a long, tough audit. Was the world a lot better-off because I helped certify a company's financial statements? I wondered whether I would eventually find a monotony in public accounting and gradually lose my interest. At the same time, the senior partner received a call from W.W. McCallum, CEO of John Morrell & Company, requesting permission to talk to me about the position of controller for the company. "Mac," as he liked to be called, was the first outsider to run the company, which had been headed by different Morrell family members for over a hundred years. The company went on the NYSE exchange in the late twenties and was the fourth largest meat packer in the world with annual sales of over $300 million.

Although profitable, the company's results had been impacted in recent years by labor difficulties at its Ottumwa, Iowa plant. The family management team concluded that an experienced outsider might be able to deal with those problems more effectively, and Mac took over as CEO in 1954. He left a senior position at Oscar Mayer Company, a smaller meat packer in size but an industry leader in profitability. I had gotten to know Mac pretty well during the 1954 audit. He was definitely a doer and a shaker, and I could see that he was intent on making the company grow. He assured me that I would be a key player on his team, and he offered an excellent package of salary, stock options, bonus, and other perks. I had been on the Morrell audit in some capacity for seven years, so I was no stranger to the company. They were great people and the meat business was fascinating—the kind that gets in your blood and stays with you.

After reflecting on these two offers for a few days, I was positive that to become controller of John Morrell & Company would be a more satisfying career for me. In a few weeks I was saying farewell, but not goodbye, to some great associates at Price Waterhouse. I was very grateful for the experiences and friendships over those seven years. Understandably, I left with some mixed emotions, but I was confidant and excited about the new opportunity with John Morrell & Company.

Chapter 17

Into the Land of the Meat Packer

Background and the First Year

John Morrell & Company was a very respected name in the meat industry with a long history dating back to 1827 when it was organized as a food and meat company in England. As agriculture and farming began to grow and flourish in America, it became a vital source of supplies for meat hungry countries like the United Kingdom. This led to Morrell's establishment of large slaughtering and meat processing plants in America's heartland—Ottumwa, Iowa, in 1877, Sioux Falls, South Dakota, in 1909, and Topeka, Kansas, in 1931. As America's population grew, the meat production from these plants gradually increased in domestic markets, and very little was exported to the United Kingdom. In Morrell's case, the American operation eventually became the parent company, and the original parent in England became a relatively small subsidiary when Morrell stock went onto the NYSE in 1928. Morrell's Midwest plants grew in concert with the increase in our country's population and the demand for meat products. As an example, when I joined Morrell in 1955, the two largest plants at Ottumwa and Sioux Falls each had about 3,000 employees and annually produced upwards of 500 million pounds of edible meat products. These large Midwestern plants supplied numerous processing and distribution branches in nearly all major metropolitan markets in the United States. Smaller markets were served by "car route" salesmen, which was a unique marketing approach developed by Morrell. It worked as follows: Orders were called into the Midwest plants, filled and shipped in a refrigerated rail car to the salesmen's headquarters, the rail car was unloaded, and deliveries were made to customers by local truck drivers. Territories were established on the basis that a salesman could sell enough meat products to fill a railroad car (30,000 pounds) weekly. At the sales level of 30,000 pounds, the gross margin would cover the delivery, salesman's salary, car and travel, and leave enough operating margin to ensure a very good bottom line return. This was certainly true for the Sioux Falls plant that made pretax income of three to four million on sales in a range of $100-$125 million. The company's Ottumwa plant was another story. On the same level of sales, the car- route marketing profits were more than offset by enormous unnecessary costs and expenses of plant operations resulting in an annual pretax loss of over one million. The plant losses were all traceable to the doorsteps of the local union. Unauthorized and illegal strikes, work stoppages, switching of delivery labels, and product sabotage were commonplace, along with many other tactics that were adverse to company profits. As mentioned earlier, the number one priority when Mac took over the reins as CEO was to develop programs and strategies that would bring Ottumwa's operations up to a profitable level.

The corporate offices of Morrell were in Ottumwa, Iowa, a sleepy town of about 35,000 situated approximately 90 miles southeast of the state's capital city of Des Moines. Having spent the first twenty years of my life in La Salle, Illinois, a community of comparable size, settling down in Ottumwa was not a total culture shock. Although there was a real scarcity of first-rate apartments, I was lucky to arrive in town when a rare vacancy suddenly was available in the city's best apartment building. Within a week, I was comfortably settled in an attractive apartment outfitted from A to Z with all new furnishings picked out by a sharp local interior decorator. I was also able to join the town's country club, which was the hub of the town's social activities. Other than private clubs, there was virtually no nightlife in Iowa during the fifties. Liquor was not sold by the drink, only by the bottle in state liquor stores. The handful of nightlifers would carry their bottles in brown bags to restaurants and key clubs that would serve setups. Accordingly, the social life and entertainment activities were all carried out in private clubs or house parties. In Ottumwa, the sidewalks were literally rolled up after dark.

My first official day of work was an easy date to remember, March 15th. I remember quite well that my first official act as an officer of the company was to sign an IRS form requesting an extension of time for the filing of the Corporation Federal Income Tax Return. Having done the company's audit for a number of years, I knew that the company's income tax procedures and administration were not good, and I had the green light from the CEO to straighten these out and get the open years settled with the IRS by the end of the current fiscal year. The company's general accounting systems, chart of accounts, and system of management reports were satisfactory, but their system of departmental accounting and transfer pricing needed major surgery. I knew that I would have plenty of work ahead to unscramble some of these important functions of the controller's office. This is a good example of why clients frequently hire their auditors to fill key posts in the controller and financial departments—their experience and familiarity with the company enables them to tackle the problems quickly and efficiently without wasting many months of orientation and learning the job.

I was on the job less than a month when the CEO reaffirmed that I was going to be a key player in his management team—a team that would take Morrell out of its doldrums and get it on the move. This would be accomplished first by a series of aggressive acquisitions of regional smaller meat companies throughout the United States. This strategic move would reduce the corporation's dependence on its huge Ottumwa plant, and therefore give it more muscle and bargaining power in negotiations with the tough labor union representing Ottumwa plant employees. I learned that I would also be the unofficial acquisition and merger manager and would work with the CEO and our general counsel in putting deals together—an exciting part of a CFO's job that I welcomed with open arms. I also learned that I would attend the regular monthly meeting of the board of directors, and present a financial and operating report.

The company filed its income tax returns with the IRS office in Ottumwa, which reported to the district office in Des Moines, which in turn reported to the regional office in Omaha. This three-dimensional tier was a nightmare in settling issues, and it lead to many open years. Rightfully the CEO hated this uncertainty of the company's federal tax picture, and he came up with a great idea. What if we moved the corporate office to Chicago? Only a few employees would be involved, and we could then file our income taxes there and get current on the open years. Moreover, moving the corporate offices to Chicago would send a message to the local union that the plant was now just another plant in Morrell's directory. In addition, the absence of corporate people would probably help the Ottumwa plant management do a better job since they wouldn't have corporate personnel looking over their shoulder. The board heartily approved the plan of the corporate office change, and it was announced immediately. A few months later the offices of the CEO, treasurer, and controller were moved to the new corporate headquarters in downtown Chicago. It remained a small group for five or six years. At that time, corporate operating and marketing offices were also moved to the corporate headquarters. Even then, it was still a relatively small group of about twenty-five employees including clerks and secretaries.

Concurrently with the usual controllership responsibilities and federal income tax problems, I worked extensively on a special assignment from the CEO, calling for an evaluation of a recent restructuring of Morrell's Dog Food Division. Morrell pioneered the formulation and production of canned dog food in the late twenties. At the outset of World War II its Red Heart brand was the most popular in the country, at which time there was a government moratorium on canned dog food production in order to conserve the supply of tin for defense purposes. Following the war, dog food production was resumed, and Red Heart quickly regained its position as number one in sales. Although the wartime moratorium made it much easier for some other competitors to close the gap. Up until this time, Red Heart had been sold by the company's meat salesmen and was a part of the total product line, which was offered to the grocery store during their weekly sales call. That way of marketing had been accepted for years. After the war, the national food chains proliferated in great numbers and basically took over the lion's share of the food business, leaving only a small amount for mom and pop corner grocery stores and small specialty deli's, etc. As the chains grew, they experienced many changes in how they operated. The purchasing function was centralized at corporate offices, leaving little real buying at the store level. Moreover, the big chain stores at that time were divided into two parts, the meat department and the grocery department, each with separate buying directions and responsibilities. This meant that the meat salesmen had to call on two people when he made his weekly calls. It was an unworkable scheme that lead to a restructuring of the entire Red Heart division. The Red Heart Dog Food products were taken from the meat salesmen's line, and all sales were turned over to established independent food brokers working out of regional warehouses.

On the production side, Morrell also made a dramatic change. Inasmuch as canned dog food was 76% water, it was an economic waste to incur an inordinate level of freight expense to ship water across the country. The solution was to arrange for Red Heart Dog Food to be produced only by regional canners throughout the United States under a cost plus basis. Because of the lower labor rates in the canning factories, the final cost, including a fair profit for the canner, was less than the production and delivery cost at the company's Midwest packing plants, which heretofore had been the sole producer of Red Heart Dog Food.

The changes in the production and marketing of Red Heart Dog Food mandated the establishment of a separate division and profit center that could be the means of a continual evaluation of its operation. The small accounting and marketing offices were established in downtown Chicago, and it was not a difficult accounting task to set up the controls to monitor the sales and marketing functions such as price list adherence, promotional allowances, co-op advertising, rebates, etc. The evaluation of the production operations by the five outside canners was not as easy. Each was a relatively small company and not steeped in good record keeping procedures for production activities. My task was to assure that the canners were producing the finished dog food in strict accordance with the formula.

On my first trip to one of the regional canners, I worked out purchasing and stock ledger inventory procedures for every item in the formula along with a means of reconciling all raw material purchases with finished production, both in terms of quantities and dollars. The other elements of cost, labor and overhead, were not significant and were relatively easy to check. Moreover, we had a contract clause that such costs would be the lower of actual or "x," so we had protection on the upside if the canner was careless in expense management.

The procedures developed at the first plant worked out quite well and became the model for all other contract canners to follow. As I went from plant to plant, I received the benefit of production experience because it was necessary to spend a good amount of time in the plant working with production people. By the time I got to the last plant, I was fairly versed in dog food production and procedures. The last plant was a very modern facility on the West Coast, but after spending less than half a day, I knew we had real trouble with the plant operator. Among other things, he was not following the formula, and he had buried all kinds of personal expenses for travel, escort services, etc., in the account for material purchases. When confronted with these matters, he blamed the formula deviation on a foreman who was to be discharged, and the improper inclusion of personal expenses in material costs as an honest error by an outside accounting service. There were many other things that added up to a clear picture of the clever operator including a myriad of personal expenses in the reimbursable cost to produce canned dog food. What to do? The plant had the capabilities to be a very efficient producer, and we needed a West Coast source of supply. A meeting on this problem was held in the CEO's office promptly upon my return. The senior partner from one of Chicago's prestigious law firms was in the meeting because the CEO (Mac) wanted the lawyer (Herb) to draw up a contract that would keep the West Coast canner in a straight jacket and ensure that we would receive quality production at an efficient cost of manufacturing. I'll never forget Herb's reply: "Mac, you've been around long enough and have made enough deals to know that all of the contract language in the world isn't going to change a crook. No matter how tough a contract I write, it won't work without a policeman." So that is exactly what we did. One of our dog food production specialists from the Ottumwa plant was transferred to the West Coast canning plant where he worked as a watchdog throughout all of the subsequent years, which were characterized by good quality production, and at efficient manufactured costs.

From my perspective, this was a very interesting special assignment. For one thing, it was an example of using accounting experience in a very positive way to achieve a controlled business operation from what had been chaos. But more importantly, the lesson learned from that final West Coast contract stayed with me throughout my entire career during the many sessions with lawyers in drafting contracts, merger and acquisition agreements, etc. Namely, tough contract language in itself will not work; there has to be a clear willingness on the part of principals to carry out the contract provisions with integrity.

As I completed my first year with the company, it was interesting to reflect on the challenging and exciting assignments and how quickly the year whizzed by. It was also an eye opener that getting along with people and having good communications were the most important stepping stones to achieve success in dealing with marketing and production. These are the two fundamental areas of business where profits are made or lost, and where accounting knowhow can be the guiding light. It was in those areas where I made the most significant contributions to the company and also where I received the greatest amount of job satisfaction. Required custodial controllership responsibilities, such as SEC and tax matters, were all important and also challenging, but they did not produce the same feeling as being a key player on the team that was building a better company.

Growing through Acquisitions

The meat packing industry is multifaceted. By its very nature, the processing of food is a fascinating tale, starting with the live animal, through many processes, and finally ending its way as a savory centerpiece on the dining room table. Yes, it is true. The meat packer uses every part of the slaughtered animal except the squeal. The huge packing plants in America's heart-land built in the early part of this century were a hallmark of plant layout and efficiency and served as a role model for Henry Ford's mass production assembly line technique. Despite these auspicious beginnings, the meat packing industry fought uphill battles in trying to achieve sustained profitability. There were constant problems indigenous to the supply and price level of livestock caused by weather and our country's agricultural policies. This in turn caused wide fluctuations in the retail prices of finished meat products that at all times compete with the poultry and fish industries for the family's food dollar. Moreover, after World War II the big labor unions representing the auto, steel, and electrical industries were able to negotiate labor agreements calling for substantial increases in labor rates, vacations, pensions, insurance, etc. Those agreements became a sort of norm that the meat packing unions were able to successfully negotiate with the major meat companies. The smaller meat companies simply did not have the financial capability for that level of labor cost. The unions knew it and were content to settle for a "sweetheart contract" calling for a much lower labor rate and fringe benefits. The effect of course made it difficult for the big companies to compete in the market place against smaller firms with favorable labor cost. An obvious strategy might have been for the big meat packer to control its marketing through its own retail markets. But this along with other expansion possibilities were barred by a "Consent Decree" with the U.S. Justice Department and agreed to by the major packers back in the mid-twenties. Because of all these factors, many firms in the industry languished in poor operating results and inadequate cash flow needed to replace worn out and obsolete facilities. Consequently, many meat companies were available for purchase in the late fifties and early sixties. They were usually available at a healthy discount from book value for a bargain price. Now add to that a federal tax code, which at the time was very favorable for corporate mergers and acquisitions, and you had a scenario that was letter perfect for Morrell's strategy of acquiring regional firms with good brand names. In doing so, the company was decreasing its dependence on the big unprofitable Ottumwa plant and at the same time adding important sales of profitable brand products to its consolidated total.

For me at least, corporate mergers and acquisitions were always exciting. For certain, each deal had a uniqueness about it, plenty of challenges, and assuredly a lot of time and hard work. But after it was signed, sealed, and delivered, there was always a good feeling of accomplishment, and among the players on our acquisition team, some very memorable camaraderie. It was through mergers and acquisitions that Morrell sales grew from $300 million in the mid-fifties to about a billion dollars twelve years later. Mac, Morrell's CEO, loved deal making and established a reputation as being fair and honest at the negotiating table and always willing to explore the possibilities. Every deal started with this pattern: Mac and the CEO of an interested seller would have a friendly luncheon or telephone discussion about the conceptual merits of a deal for both companies. (Not once were business brokers or investment deal makers involved. Sometimes Mac initiated the contact but more frequently the prospective seller contacted Mac.) If this initial contact produced a serious interest and a green light to proceed, Mac would shortly receive a package of financial, marketing, and operating information from the seller. Mac would give the data a cursory review, call me for a meeting in which he outlined the developments-to-date, and we would jointly brainstorm the sellers information package.

Due to our reputation, we were bombarded with many offers and turned down most of them after this first review. However, if an offer looked promising, my responsibility was to make a further and more detailed review of the data and then construct some financial models under several sets of assumptions, i.e., the seller's asking price, marketing and operating trends, projections, etc. I could usually do these models in a day or two and then meet with Mac to review my findings and recommendations. If the transaction looked like a good fit, Mac would immediately call the CEO of the seller and discuss the next steps—arrangements for plant visits, the need for more marketing data, or whatever. If we concluded that the transaction did not meet our criteria, Mac would nevertheless call the CEO of the seller and in a friendly way explain why and thank them for their cooperation. Mac was never keen on cold, stereotypical business letters. The acquisitions that we made fell into two distinct categories.

Purchase of Assets

If the selling company did not have a usable tax loss, we would buy for cash the land and depreciable assets, usually at a healthy discount, and the inventories based on a current physical that was observed by our personnel and our outside auditors. We never purchased the seller's accounts receivables, but we as agent turned over any subsequent collections to the seller. Nor did we assume any liabilities other than those covered by statute or existing contracts of the seller, i.e., the labor agreement covering plant workers.

Purchase of Stock

If the selling company had a usable tax loss, we would acquire the seller's stock and by keeping the business "as is" for two years, we could use the seller's pre-acquisition tax losses in our then current consolidated federal income tax return. In this kind of acquisition we were stepping into the seller's shoes with respect to all assets and liabilities—those on the books and those that might not be recorded. Accordingly it was incumbent on us to make a thorough review of the seller's statements and to provide in the contract adequate warranties by the seller, as well as holding some of the purchase price in escrow to cover unrecorded liabilities. (Note: Congress has since tightened the tax code and regulations covering the use of tax loss carryforwards and carry-backs so that it is virtually impossible to repeat this tax strategy that we successfully employed in the mid-fifties and early sixties.)

Whether we purchased assets or stock, it was always an accounting rat race to cut off the seller's business one day (the effective acquisition date) and start fresh records on the next business day for the new owner—Morrell. To accommodate the transition of the business, a good deal of common sense planning was required in order that the transition would be smooth and without any disruptive effect on the seller's workforce. But it was also most important that the outside world, customers, suppliers, and others be notified in a way that enhanced the seller's image and assured the continuity and the established good will of all its business relationships.

My corporate responsibilities included the management of all acquisitions. Depending on the size and expected complications of the transaction, I would bring along others on my staff as were required. Normally it would take about two weeks to do all the things that were needed yesterday—like pricing the physical inventory and settling any and all controversial issues with the seller in order to meet the deadline for the usual second closing. In this connection it might be well to point out that sometimes the acquisition agreement is drafted by a lawyer who doesn't even know Accounting 101 (but thinks they know accounting from A to Z.) The word of caution here is to make certain that the CFO reviews the final draft of the proposed contract and approves the language covering all accounting related matters.

The first few weeks after the acquisition is a sort of honeymoon period during which the buyer and seller get to know each other and hopefully establish a good working rapport. An acquisition manager for the buyer need not be an accounting genius. Instead they need to wear many hats and orchestrate the agreement and understanding of the principals in a clear and friendly way. This is not the time or place for spurious accuracy or a hard-nosed and conceited attitude in handling such matters as changeovers to new and different company policies. This honeymoon period is probably even more important to the buyer because it affords some opportunity to evaluate the new acquisition's most important assets that are not on the books—the human assets. In the span of four or five weeks you would get a pretty good impression of the quality and capabilities of the management staff through the numerous meetings and discussions that are a normal and necessary part of this post acquisition indoctrination. When everything had settled down we always concluded the transaction with an elegant dinner party (spouses included) for the new division's management staff and the senior officers of Morrell. Mac always did a sincere and effective job of welcoming everyone on board, and he established a friendly atmosphere for good working relationships.

I was involved in over twenty-five acquisitions during my thirteen years at Morrell and while each deal had a lot of similarities, every deal had something a little different, and most of the time the difference was an issue that was never contemplated by the parties—it just came out of the woodwork. Let me tell you about one of my more memorable acquisitions.

Morrell operated two first-class processing branches in California, Los Angeles and Oakland. In that huge Bay Area growth market we had the opportunity to buy a prominent San Francisco service truck operation featuring deli-meats and other specialty deli foods. We also had the opportunity to buy an Oakland meat company that featured a broad line of processed meats and more importantly, a prominent, first-class hotel and restaurant supply division. Morrell had no deli-meat or hotel and restaurant supply operations anywhere in its vast array of meat operations. These acquisitions would be perfect for acquiring the knowhow, and incorporating these in other plants that served the larger metropolitan markets in the country. These companies became available very quickly, and Mac had to do a solo job in working out all the contract details in San Francisco. He called me with the simple message: "Pack a bag for a couple of weeks and get on the next plane to San Francisco." It was Wednesday and both deals were to become effective Saturday. When I met Mac the next morning, I learned of a blockbuster problem surfacing for each deal. Maybe it was the trauma of selling the business, but at any rate the owner of the deli business was admitted to a psychiatric hospital for severe mental depression. The purchase contract had been quickly drafted for the purchase of the assets and the business, but many other important business matters and loose ends were to be negotiated and settled with him before the second closing. Meanwhile the stockholders of the Oakland company sold all of their stock to the alleged head of the West Coast Mafia. We were now dealing with an unknown who didn't know anything about a meat business. Moreover, the proposed transaction had a lot of loose ends that had to be taken care of and negotiated between the contract date and the second closing—some three to four weeks later. Counsel for the deli company was a San Francisco law firm, and we worked out a satisfactory agreement to proceed with the deal and extend the second closing to a reasonable date after the deli owner was discharged from the hospital. With respect to the Oakland deal, our counsel advised us that we had no alternative except to continue with the deal. The only difference now being that we had to settle a lot of business matters with a person unknown to us, with a reputation that was very suspect.

I borrowed personnel from our Oakland branch, and we carried out all the usual accounting matters required under the two agreements, i.e., taking and pricing the inventories, sales and purchase cutoffs, bank account changes, establishing new ledgers ad infinitum. In a few days we had a lot of these matters under control and well under way, and it was time for me to contact the new owner of the Oakland company about settling the numerous loose ends of the contract. When I called him I heard a very raspy but cordial voice. "How about lunch tomorrow?" he asked. I agreed, and the next day I met "Mr. G" for the first time. What I saw was a perfect Godfather—a man in his fifties about six feet-two with a very athletic build. Even though he was bald, he was a good looking man with classic Italian features. He was dressed like a fashion plate replete with a Borsolino hat and a huge diamond on his ring finger. After we introduced each other he said, "Let's just go to lunch today. I'm very busy and we'll talk business later on." His personal chauffeur and limo were waiting to take us to one of San Francisco's top restaurants. When he paid the lunch tab it was with fresh currency—he had a phobia about even touching circulated currency. When he dropped me off at the office, I was pretty certain he was the West Coast Mafia boss and if he wasn't, he was a perfect impostor.

We met about every other day, working and cleaning up contract items that had to be settled by the parties, i.e., proration of various liabilities, sales and purchases commitments, and employee benefit matters. We got along fine. Although he was a stranger in contract matters he had good common sense and was enjoying these negotiations. He was a likeable guy, but nevertheless I was a bit leery about him. I always addressed him as Mr.

G and never once conceded anything. In a few weeks we finally came to the last item—what we would pay for the physical inventory. The contract language essentially said cost or market, whichever lower, but the language used to describe how to figure cost or market was in very complicated legalese. For this matter Mr. G brought along his accountant, who had little experience in this kind of transaction. There was considerable market appreciation in many of the freezer inventory stocks, and the accountant was trying to understand this and explain it to his boss. It was the blind leading the blind. Finally Mr. G slammed his fist on the table, pointed his finger in his accountant's face, and in his raspy voice shouted "You keepa yo mout shut or tomorrow you'll be swimmin' in San Francisco Bay with cement shoes on." His accountant's pleasant expression turned to one of terror; for me it was a tense situation, and I responded instantly. I put my hand on Mr. G's shoulder, flashed him a bit of a smile, looked him dead in the eye and said, "Gam" (the only time I ever called him by his nickname) "don't be so tough on Phil. He was only trying to help you. This contract is very complicated. Let me go through this inventory section with you, and I'll show you how it works." He relaxed and for the next half hour, he listened to a combination of Accounting 101, why acquisition legalese is necessary, and my own sermon on the mount on business integrity. When I finished he said, "Okay, we do the deal like it says." It was a happy ending to a very thorny situation, and financially speaking we were able to realize the inventory market appreciation and start the new operations with a windfall of about $100,000. I've often wondered if Mr. G was half kidding or serious about his accountant swimming in the San Francisco Bay, but as things worked out, I'll never know. At that meeting we wrapped everything up, and I thought it was my last meeting with Mr. G. But it wasn't. A couple of days later, he called me for lunch to talk about a personal matter. Would you believe he wanted me to become his personal business manager, and he offered me an incredible financial arrangement. Nevertheless, there was not enough money in the world to even tempt me to make that affiliation. However, I had to be diplomatic, careful, and delicate in framing my negative response. It wasn't easy, but he finally accepted it and we parted on a friendly note. Whew!!

Meanwhile the acquisitions of the deli had proceeded smoothly. I had been splitting my time evenly between the two deals, and I was also acting as a general manager while the owner was in the hospital. In a few weeks he was released, and he looked like a million when he stopped by the plant on his first day home. He acted and talked like a man on cloud nine and was very eager to return to the plant the next morning for full-time work. That evening he took his life. It was a terrible loss to the company because he was a marketing whiz and was destined to become a senior officer on Morrell's corporate staff. Sadly, business had to continue, and it became my job to settle the many contract loose ends with his lawyer who was very capable and fair. Understandably, it took longer because he was not familiar with many aspects of the business nor of oral understandings as to operations and other business matters. However, in a few weeks everything was buttoned up, and I was able to bring back a complete set of financial statements to Mac for our new Bay Area Division—mission accomplished thanks to hard work and long hours from a great group of staff members.

The British expression "the proof of the pudding is in the eating" is one of my favorites because it is perfectly simplistic and absolute. In a similar way, the proof of an extensive acquisition program is in the bottom line. In Morrell's case the financial markets liked the aggressive acquisition program that produced record sales and earnings from the mid-fifties to the mid-sixties that sent Morrell stock soaring from around $9 per share to record highs in the 30-40 dollar range. Conclusion: for the relatively short-term the acquisition program was very successful because it added a hefty amount of net income to the company's financial statement, and the presence of many new company plants was a factor in a wholesome change of attitude by the Ottumwa plant union. This led to a turnaround of what had been a very unprofitable plant. However, it is not possible to assess the long-term impact of the acquisition program because, as explained later in this chapter, Morrell was one of the many companies sold or merged in an astounding period of takeovers in the meat industry that took place in the late sixties.

Rebuilding the Accounting System

As mentioned earlier in this chapter, Morrell's general accounting system that I had seen and worked with as an outside auditor was reasonably satisfactory. But as Morrell started to grow quickly through acquisitions, it became quite apparent that major surgery was needed on the total accounting and information systems. To do this timely and correctly I was fortunate enough to hire two top professionals from Price Waterhouse—Frank Hianik and Bill O'Meara. I had worked with them at Price Waterhouse and knew that they had the technical skills and personalities for the job. Besides, each had considerable exposure and experience with the meat industry.

They started on my staff as elected officers and from day one the three of us functioned as a smooth and efficient team. My technical focus covered mergers and acquisitions, federal and state taxes, planning, and computer administrations. Frank's area of concentration was the financial side of the business—banking and cash management, insurance, pensions, credit and vehicle administration; Bill's area of concentration was general accounting, costs, and operational accounting. The three of us frequently interchanged work responsibilities and pitched in wherever a body was needed. During the period of all the deals and mergers, my financial department was in a constant state of up-tempo activity. One day a fellow corporate officer was in my department, and after observing the frenzied work pace remarked, "You guys work like Indians—you must be Comanches!" That remark spawned a nickname in our low key and congenial corporate office group. The controller's staff became known as the Comanches.

There is a lot more to a chart of accounts than a mere array of account numbers and account names. It is absolutely essential that instructions are complete as to how each account works, i.e., when it is debited or credited and why. Accordingly, this eliminates guess work when decisions have to be made regarding entries in the general records. Understandably, the chart of accounts is often the second step in developing the system—the first step being the policies that embrace every phase of the company's operations. The language of the company policies will govern what accounts are to be used and how they will operate. Morrell's official policy manual was incomplete and needed an overhaul to accommodate the newer and bigger Morrell. Since so many of the policies had financial and accounting implications, we inherited the responsibility as authors and editors of the newly named "Corporate Orders," that was issued with a new look and a new everything, including orders with no immediate accounting impact, but that were extremely important, such as broad company policies dealing with human resources, integrity, behavior, and corporate objectives. The Corporate Orders were classified according to these categories:

1) General Administrative
2) Operations
3) Marketing
4) Financial and Accounting

Our first priority, of course, was to update or draft orders covering financial and accounting areas, followed by the orders for administrative operations and marketing that impacted the financial records. The order that had number one priority for us was that covering "Intercompany Transactions." With our many plants, branches, and subsidiary companies doing so much business with each other, balancing the intercompany accounts had been a constant bugaboo that delayed the prompt issuance of monthly financial statements. Frank spearheaded this one and worked out a foolproof self-balancing procedure that assured that the intercompany accounts would automatically balance and therefore "eliminate" in the monthly consolidating statements. The order included among other things a numerical control by the issuer and cutoff instructions so that every unit would know when it had all of its intercompany charges. It was mandatory that the receiving unit had to record the intercompany charge even though it may have had good reason to question it (sort of like record it now and fight later) and finally, a confirming phone call by each unit after their first preliminary closing to check out their intercompany balances. This order worked like a charm and was the key to closing the books for a flash profit and loss report to the CEO on the fifth business day after the monthly closing. Considering the computer technology of the fifties, this closing period of five business days was remarkable. Some of the other orders that we drafted in order to expedite monthly closings dealt with:

1) The payables, the instructions for cutoffs, and estimates
2) Depreciation reserves
3) Physical inventory adjustments
4) Bad debt reserves
5) Annualized corporate charge for insurance and other head office administrative expenses
6) Capital and repair appropriations ledger

In rewriting the chart of accounts, the instructions on how to use the accounts followed the precise language of the Corporate Orders to the letter. Examples of Corporate Orders covering administrative, operations, and marketing with accounting and chart of account implications are:

1) *Administrative.* The company formed a foundation to use for all charitable contributions on behalf of the corporation and all of its divisions. However, small local expenditures to the Boy Scouts, etc., could be paid by the local divisions as a public relations expense. The rules for this were spelled out in the Orders.

2) *Operations.* The broad corporate policies as they pertained to personnel and employee benefits touched many areas with numerous expense requirements—i.e., vacations, holidays, sick leave, moving expenses, etc., with instructions as to what, if any, exceptions might apply to local management.

3) *Marketing.* The policies governing the use of an automobile for the hundreds of company salesmen, as well as personal use, expenses, trade-ins, replacements, etc., were spelled out as to the degree of local involvement and corporate control and supervision.

Upon the completion of the Corporate Orders and a revised chart of accounts, we were able to hand over these items to a newly acquired unit, and like an encyclopedia, the Orders literally provided answers to all the questions the acquired unit might have regarding their new affiliation with Morrell. The Corporate Orders were extremely helpful to the company's internal auditors, and their field work included audit programs and tests to ascertain that all Corporate Orders were being followed.

The new chart of accounts was constructed and planned so that account group totals would flow directly to the format of our published financial statements, and no account reclassifications or any account analysis were required. This was a big help internally and also to our outside accountants for the annual audit.

There is one final step in our rebuilding of the system, and that was the establishment of uniform, management operating and marketing reports to be used by all divisions. We started with some very excellent reports coming out of the data processing departments at Ottumwa and Sioux Falls. We modified these somewhat so that newly acquired divisions could also prepare these reports without a prohibitive degree of changes. When this was accomplished, we had a first-rate score card on how each of the many divisions performed in so many vital categories such as livestock procurement, production yields, expense control, product line profitability, etc. These reports were absolutely necessary in the meat industry, which traditionally enjoys very high sales but very low gross margins. It enabled management to spot any poor performances and take immediate action. As you will read in later chapters, realistic and accurate comparable financial data is a very important tool for management.

Controls at Work: A Case History

An effective system of internal control is designed to provide reasonable assurance that the company's assets are safeguarded and that all transactions are properly recorded and executed in accordance with the company's policies. Morrell's family of divisions and subsidiaries was large enough to permit the usual separation of duties and the necessary checks and balances inherent in a good internal control system. However, all of this is for naught if there is collusion among employees who know the system and conspire to abscond with company assets. Such was the case at a major subsidiary that slaughtered hogs and also produced a very successful line of processed canned meats. The controls employed for the slaughter operation were basic.

1) Hogs were weighed going to the kill floor.
2) The dressed carcasses were weighed again when they were transferred from the kill floor to the cutting department.
3) The individual pork cuts were then weighed when they were transferred from the cutting department to the fresh meat cooler.
4) Transfers to processing departments or to the shipping department for fresh pork sale were all weighed.
5) At the end of the work day, all transfers in and out were matched up and balanced, and a daily production report was prepared. At the end of the week these were summarized and sent to the corporate office.
6) At the corporate office these reports from all slaughtering plants were carefully analyzed, particularly the yield of all the individual cuts, i.e., hams, butts, bellies, ribs, etc.

Shortly after being acquired, they began reporting their weekly hog slaughtering and cutting activity according to the Morrell format. A comparative analysis then indicated that the rib yield was running about 1½ % from this new subsidiary whereas the yield was closer to 2% at all other plants—a variation that was explained by local management as the result of cutting the ribs differently to accommodate their type of customer. It appeared to be a reasonable explanation, and that's the way the matter remained for a number of years. Then a most unusual change occurred one summer month with respect to the rib yield percentage on the weekly production report from this subsidiary—it jumped from its customary number of about 1½% to 2%. This happened for three consecutive weeks and then the yield returned to the "historic" yield of about 1½%. Investigation followed and a bizarre defalcation was uncovered. Here's how it worked.

About four or five employees were in the scheme—key employees of the fresh meat cooler, the shipping foreman, and the gate guard. Each day the foremen of the cutting department would set aside a number of 100-pound barrels of ribs and not include these in the production weights for the day. These would be earmarked in a special way, and the set aside weight was not included in weight transfer reports as the ribs moved in and out of the fresh meat cooler and finally to the shipping department where the foreman filled orders to the customer, who was also part of the scheme and who picked up shipments daily. Example: The barrels set aside (say there were four) would not be included in the billing. The customer would receive say fourteen barrels but the invoice would show only ten. Since the gate guard and trucker were also in on the deal it was no problem to the "gang" to get the unbilled quantities out the gate and into the hands of the customer. Ultimately the customer kicked back cash to the gang based on an agreed percentage of the fair market value of the stolen property.

The defalcation was uncovered when the regular foreman of the cutting department took his annual vacation. He always handpicked the employee to be acting foreman while he was on vacation. This time, however, the replacement got sick, and the plant manager had one of his assistants take over. Of course the temporary foreman weighed all of the pork cuts and didn't set any aside. This resulted in the rib yields jumping suddenly to about 2% like all of the other slaughtering plants. This was followed up promptly, and a very intensive investigation was conducted. Aided by outside detectives and complete and accurate records, we were able to prove a loss of almost $500,000, most of which was recovered from the insurance company.

There are three lessons to be learned from this case history:

1) Collusion by the right employees can probably beat any system of internal control if they don't get too greedy.
2) Our production group should have taken a "show me" stance when the new subsidiary explained why the rib yields were lower.
3) In the final analysis, the defalcation was uncovered because the management information system that we designed was con-

stantly monitoring the production side of the business and brought to light a condition that led to the ultimate disclosure of the defalcation.

El Gerente (Manager)—a.k.a. "Señor K"

I acquired a new temporary title in 1964 as manager of the company's El Paso plant, which had been acquired two years earlier. The plant workforce of about 500 employees was largely Mexican and each workday, crossed the bridge spanning the Rio Grande river that divides El Paso, Texas and Juarez, Mexico. The announcement of my appointment as general manager was posted on the bulletin boards in Spanish; a small English version was also posted. The Spanish speaking workforce had trouble with my Polish surname, but Señor "K" was a most agreeable substitute. This was a very interesting experience in my career.

At about this time I had started to lose the enthusiasm and satisfaction for my job in Chicago. It just wasn't fun anymore. Among other things, I was not able to install a much needed corporate strategic plan. ("It will work in other companies but not the meat industry," is what I kept hearing.) Moreover, my appraisal of the future of the company was starting to look bearish. We were looking at some upcoming sizeable write-offs for certain acquisitions and projects, and all of them had been engineered by the corporate operations chief. As long as his myopic and penny-pinching philosophy prevailed, the company was heading in the wrong direction. This is what I told Mac, our CEO, and gave for the reasons I was thinking about resigning. He pleaded with me not to, and asked me to go to El Paso and to straighten out a colossal mess. It was very appealing to me because it would give me a chance to prove I was more than a "number dummy." At the time, I was a bachelor and had no family ties, but I had plenty of roots and interests in Chicago. I did not want to accept the position unless I could return to Chicago for one week each month and stay in El Paso no longer than six months. This would bring me back to the corporate office in time to direct the annual closing of the company's books and records. Mac agreed to this, and my El Paso odyssey was underway.

The El Paso plant was a full-scale meat plant, slaughtering hogs, cattle, and lambs and processing sausage, bacon, and smoked hams. It was a good plant and its products enjoyed a fine reputation in the burgeoning southwestern markets. It was profitable when we bought it and continued to be profitable until the founder's health failed, and he had to step down. His son, who succeeded him was smart and a likeable man after working hours, but during the workday he was a failure. Under his helm, the monthly operating results gradually turned sour and worsened each month to loss levels that were severe.

From day one, everything involved with the El Paso assignment seemed to click and fall in the right place. On the very first day I found an excellent furnished apartment across from Texas Western University (now called UTEP). On my first day at the plant, I interviewed every department manager and key employee, and I could not have been happier with the team I inherited. They were talented in their field and quite eager to help to get the plant back on its feet. I didn't need to give them any motivational speeches like Notre Dame's Knute Rockne's famous halftime plea to "Go out there and win one for the Gipper." All my team needed was leadership and support, and I assured them that they would get a full measure of both.

Having directed the acquisition of this company two years earlier as well as the conversion to Morrell's accounting and management information system, I knew that all the cost and financial data and computer programs were available to develop weekly operating and profit plans. Here is the planning program I put into place.

The Projected Product Costs

Industrial engineers had worked up the unit labor and direct expenses for all products along with the raw material specs for the product. This information was stored in the computer and the program printed an update on all product costs based on the estimated prices for livestock and primal cut values. On Wednesday morning the livestock department would provide the estimate for hog, cattle, and lamb prices for the ensuing week. These prices would be fed into the cost program, all product costs would be updated, and a run would be prepared for sales management that afternoon.

The Projected Sales Volume and Margin

The sales manager would provide a sales forecast for each item in the product line based on his knowledge of the market, the season, competition and, of course, the expected cost. This forecast would be given to data processing by noon on Thursday and tabulated for a four o'clock staff meeting that afternoon.

The Projected Weekly Bottom Line

The total profit margin shown on the sales forecast report was the starting point for arriving at the bottom line. Based on current experience and trends, and input from the department managers, I developed the total estimated expenses (direct and indirect), which would be deducted from our sales margins on our financial report at the end of the month and then adjusted to a weekly amount that was deducted from the weekly estimate of total sales margin. All of this information was looked at carefully by the entire team at the weekly Thursday afternoon meeting. We wouldn't sit still for a projection that would show a loss or a mediocre performance. Our focus was always, "How can we make it better?" And indeed it did get better, thanks to ideas and suggestions presented and developed at these meetings. After the meetings, I gave data processing all of the changes in the original estimate. These were then reflected in a final print-out that was, in effect, our total target for the coming week.

The Feed Back—Actual Compared with Plan

The meat packing week traditionally ends on Saturday, and by Tuesday morning the data processing department would have prepared a report showing the actual sales volume, costs, and sales margins for the prior week. That afternoon the team would meet again, go over all the variations from the plan, and pinpoint if possible, the reasons for major short falls.

At first, these two weekly meetings were rather lengthy, but they became shorter as the team became efficient planners and overcame their initial inexperience. They were cognizant of the effectiveness of the planning function and were elated to be part of a team that was getting the plant profitable again. Each department manager was a major contributor to the profitable comeback of the plant, but the biggest dollar impact resulted from the first meeting when we compared the actual weekly results with our plan. The sales margin total was substantially less than the plan total, and nearly all of the individual product margins were less than the plan totals. Intensive discussions brought to light the fact that sales to several of the major buying organizations were at prices significantly below the official price list for the week. The sales manager stated that this had been the plant policy for quite awhile and that we would lose the business if we changed this policy. Moreover, I learned that the prior general manager had only one benchmark for the sales department—volume. Product line profitability and total sales margins were never reviewed with the sales manager. He assumed he had been doing a good job because he maintained an acceptable sales volume. What was apparently needed was immediate surgery to change the mind-set and pricing strategies of the sales department. The "operation" took place the following morning. The pricing history and sales volume of every item in the salesmen's order book was reviewed and revised to reflect a realistic current market price, taking into account that certain products were not price sensitive because of brand loyalty and superior quality. For these, a premium selling price was established. In addition to the pricing revisions, two other sales disciplines were adopted. One was a rigid requirement of price list adherence. (A price discount or shade would require approval of the sales manager.) Two was a small order control that required that each incoming sales order total at least 100 pounds. The sales manager was really nervous about these changes and said, "I hope they work, but I'll bet two chains blow their top and drop us." He was wrong. One chain buyer did blow his top and dropped us, but only for one week. That was certainly proof positive that the plant had consumer brand loyalty, and the retail markets needed our marketing presence.

The first weekly plan following the pricing changes showed a profit, and each week thereafter we were able to improve to a level that was a very satisfactory return on our net assets and among the best in Morrell's family of plants and companies.

The plant location in El Paso was not the most ideal place for livestock supplies, and it had been necessary to supplant its weekly kill requirements with cattle from feedlots located only a few miles from the plant. The plant would systematically buy feeder cattle, fatten them up, and slaughter them when they reached optimum weight. Unfortunately, when I assumed my responsibilities as general manager, I found that far too many cattle had been purchased for feeding, and the feedlot inventory was an enormous problem. The company had over ten million dollars tied up in thousands of beef cattle, and far too many were now classified as "boarders," (a term for cattle who have passed their optimum weight and are eating their daily ration with only a minimum weight gain, resulting in a net loss on the feeding operation). I had the feedlot cowboys cull out all the obvious boarders and we went on an extended shift in our beef kill department. At this time it was pure luck to have a good carload market in the large eastern cities. This enabled us to sell off our boarders and even make some profit on the transactions. That took care of a short-term problem in feedlot operations, but many long-term revisions were still needed in the existing system in order to have full control and financial evaluation starting with the purchase of feeder cattle and ending with their value as dressed carcasses in the beef cooler according to their respective grade (i.e., prime, choice, commercial, or utility).

The physical facilities including pens, scales, and grain hopper bins, were in top condition, and it was relatively simple to keep records by pens (usually three-hundred cattle to a pen) showing the purchase date and price and the daily cost of feed consumed by pen until the animals were transferred to the kill floor. At that time the animals would be weighed and the cost per pound of gain could be determined. This was an important step because we were then able to determine which daily feed ration was best. (The feedlot had four different rations, but no tests had been made to determine which was best).

One more revision was needed, and that was the use of hedges to protect against the wide fluctuations in livestock prices which could fluctuate as much as twenty percent in a six-month period; I think you can appreciate the importance of hedging when your inventory at risk is normally around five million dollars. A hedge assured that an efficient feedlot operator would always be profitable because he would not be at risk for changes in the market prices for livestock. If the live market price for cattle increased, that profit would be offset by a loss on the hedge. Conversely, if the live market price for cattle decreased, that loss would be offset by a profit on the hedge. Morrell had a membership in the Chicago Board of Trade, and in a short time we were very active in purchasing cattle hedges.

In one of President Kennedy's early meetings with the President of Mexico, the Mexican President brought up the subject of a ninety-nine-year-old border dispute between the United States and Mexico. It happened because the Rio Grande River (the natural boundary between the U.S. and Mexico) changed its course in 1864 that resulted in a loss of 630 acres of Mexican land. This boundary dispute had been reviewed years ago by an International Tribunal that recommended that the acres be returned to Mexico, but the United States Government did nothing about it. When President Kennedy looked into this, he quickly put in motion a treaty to return this land to Mexico. Well, guess what? Our El Paso plant was situated on the far northern tip of that 630-acre tract. As a result of the treaty called El Chamizal, the U.S. government agreed to pay affected property owners the fair market value of their property and reimburse them for the costs of relocation. The target date for completing this was 1967, some three years away. My first involvement was to find a new plant site at a price that was reasonable, not an inflated price because of the impact of El Chamizal. By using nominees and knowledgeable locals, I was able to procure a perfect site for the new plant. My next involvement was to work with our general counsel and the U.S. Government Boundary Commission to negotiate and settle the amounts that we would receive for the value of the old plant and the costs to relocate. When these matters were all satisfactorily concluded, I had the highest respect for the demeanor and integrity of the government employees who handled the Chamizal matter. They were true professionals in every sense of the word.

My six-month stay whizzed by like it was six weeks, and it could not have been more enjoyable. Although the hours were long, the satisfaction of all our accomplishments in restoring plant profitability, setting up weekly sales and an operating plan, and new controls for the feedlot operations made it all worthwhile. In addition there was the diversity of situations that this veteran accountant had not experienced—like settling labor grievances with the Union, meeting with the mayor on civic matters, entertaining senior officers of our larger accounts, and last but not least, the task of finding a site for the new El Paso plant.

I returned to the corporate office to resume my regular duties, leaving behind a great management team at our now very profitable El Paso plant. I turned the reins over to a capable general manager with a very good track record at our St. Louis plant.

My El Paso odyssey was very good for the company because I found the right management combination and business strategies to turn a loser into a solid profit maker. From my own standpoint it was quite successful because it upgraded my stature on the corporate staff. But more importantly, it was a wonderful learning experience that doesn't come along very often to a CFO. My many different audits and business studies over the prior fifteen years had exposed me to all phases of a business entity, and it was my challenge to put a going business together like fitting all the pieces in a jig saw puzzle. For me it was proof that when diversified accounting experience is added to good communication skills and the ability to get along with people, the right ingredients are present for the professional accountant to successfully move into senior management positions.

Corporate Culture and Personality

This is a nonaccounting section which I could not have written twenty-five years ago. At that time I simply did not have the business experience or maturity to recognize that corporations, like humans, are all different—each possesses a distinct array of values that is the driving force in both its short- and long-term activities. It's the sum total of a company's culture and personality that makes it unique and sets it apart from the rest of the pack. But, changes in personality and values are sure to slowly occur over time. Yesterday's winners can be today's losers. Witness the 1993 difficulties of General Motors and IBM as prime examples of this. All of the reasons leading to their 1993 restructuring may never be known to the general public but it's a certainty that some of the problems had roots going back a number of years.

Looking back at the Morrell Company as an auditor and their chief accounting officer, I saw a company with the highest ideals and morality in all of its business activities and relations with employees. It enjoyed a fine reputation with customers, suppliers, and as a good corporate citizen where its plants were located. Throughout its history, the company always insisted on top quality facilities, and its large plants and processing branches were among the best in the industry. The company was operations-minded, but it was marketing driven and consequently, it was the marketing group that called the shots on new products, market research, development, and on many plant operating matters. It also had the final say on many corporate level plans.

But as pointed out in an earlier paragraph, Morrell started to grow at a quick pace in the mid-fifties via an acquisition program inaugurated by its new CEO, Wally McCallum. In a short time it became apparent that senior officers had to be added to the corporate staff to coordinate financial, operating, and marketing activities throughout Morrell's newer and bigger array of divisions and subsidiaries. Although the plant managers reported directly to the CEO, the new corporate operations group became very involved in many local plant matters as well as some of the corporate marketing and administration functions. The shift of power from marketing to operations was so gradual that it didn't really become apparent for a number of years—like the drip, drip, drip of a leaky faucet, it takes quite awhile before the room is flooded. The corporate operations chief who orchestrated these many changes was a relative newcomer with no big company or marketing experience. His personal lifestyle was very frugal, and it was also characteristic of his business thinking. Somehow he was able to sell the CEO his business philosophies, and in over a dozen years he single handedly changed the face and culture of the company. (How he managed to accomplish this is still a mystery.) A few examples, big and small include the following.

1) The important Red Heart Dog Food Division was literally taken over by operations, which became solely responsible for new product development. The dog food market was rapidly changing from a canned variety to a dry product sold in bags. Time was of the essence. Unfortunately, operations took several years to develop the new dry product. The results were disastrous. The formulation and processing procedures were wrong which resulted in both dogs and owners not liking the product. A huge inventory was dumped and the project was abandoned at a significant loss. It spelled the demise for a profitable division that was once the industry leader.

2) Many sausage and canned meat formulations and recipes were changed to reduce product costs but the result was a lessening in quality and taste, and in time, a decline in those product sales.

3) Petty cost-cutting decisions included discontinuing the monthly employee magazine, closing the public relations department (consisting of two employees), terminating The Morrell Chorus, ending distribution of the famed Morrell calendar to customers, and the cancelling of campus visits for college recruitment. The savings were small but the impact was significant.

4) The knowhow of the hotel and restaurant supply business and the peddler truck, deli operation acquired in the company's acquisition of businesses in the Bay Area, was not incorporated in a single other company division.

5) Operations became a big factor in acquisitions, and in doing so deals were made for obsolete slaughtering plants simply because they were cheap.

6) Operations personnel routinely attended used machinery auctions to buy unneeded equipment that was stored for future use.

Ad Nauseam —Ad Infinitum

The change in company culture had a telling effect on employee morale. As I mentioned earlier in this chapter, I was on the verge of resigning and I was not alone. Of course, the change brought about adverse changes in operating results. The earning momentum that Mac was able to generate in the late fifties and early sixties gradually dissipated. In 1965 the company posted its first loss in decades, followed by meager earnings in 1966-67. Naturally the earnings decline was accompanied by a drop in the market value of the stock, making the company far more vulnerable to a takeover which is described in the a later paragraph. For those of you who are just starting out in the business world, you can only be a witness on the sidelines of what is happening culture-wise in your job affiliation. Later, however, you can help change or shape your company's culture, and it will be wise if you remember its importance as I've highlighted here in Morrell's case history.

The American Meat Institute

In 1906, Congress passed the Meat Inspection Act which made federal inspection mandatory for all meat sold in interstate and foreign commerce. It was the first step in making the federal government a regulator of the meat industry, and on October first of that year the first regulations were issued. On that same date a group of meat packers met to form an association— The American Meat Institute was born. Generally, its purpose was to interact with federal regulators and legislators in Washington, D.C. on meat industry and related matters, as well as to use Institute staff personnel for industry-wide scientific research and economic studies, and meat promotion and consumer education. Since most of the larger packers were headquartered in Chicago it was only natural that the Institute established its general office in the Windy City, which enjoyed the reputation as "the hog butcher of the world." The Institute also opened an office in Washington, D.C. to carry out the usual lobbying practices of large trade associations.

When I joined Morrell in 1955 the American Meat Institute was nearing its peak in terms of membership and activity. The annual meeting held in Chicago was a week in length and attracted thousands. The meat packers literally filled every good hotel and restaurant in the city.

The Institute organization consisted of many full-time professionals, but it also drew upon industry experts to staff the numerous committees that covered every phase of the meat business. It's board of directors consisted mainly of CEOs of the leading companies in the industry.

The accounting committee of which I was a member, was a very important and active group. Nearly every other committee would come to the accounting committee for financially related advice, as well as numbers related to meat departments and livestock activities. This called for meetings with other committees and enabled me to get acquainted with many industry leaders outside of the accounting field. The time I spent on committee matters was always a learning and productive experience—never a waste of time.

I received a very pleasant surprise shortly after returning to Morrell's corporate office in Chicago, following my stint as the general manager of the company's El Paso plant. The accounting committee chairman, and my good friend, Ivan Beaman of Wilson Company had retired, and the committee elected me as his successor. I felt very honored to step into this position that earlier had been held by prominent members of the industry, and I promised to carry on the committee's successful traditions. I held the chairmanship post for several years before I left the industry, and with some marvelous committee support we were able to achieve a number of important objectives.

Objective 1

The committee had previously engaged an accounting professor to write a book on planning and control especially for the meat industry. He was a good text book writer but had no practical experience in the meat industry. Consequently, he had only completed a few chapters and his meat inexperience was apparent. To get the job done committee members finished writing the book jointly with Price Waterhouse personnel who had extensive meat industry accounting experience from their audit clients. The book was published and received many accolades from all sectors of the industry.

Objective 2

The committee established a weekly reporting system of departmental operating results for the hog kill and beef kill departments, whereby companies volunteering to participate would submit the departmental financial data to Price Waterhouse, who in turn would publish and distribute the information to the participants without identifying any company name. This was very enthusiastically received because it enabled participants to see how they fared against competition in this very important phase of meat industry. Because of the success of this reporting system for the kill departments, the committee was requested to extend the report to include branded product departments, i.e., sausage, smoked hams, sliced bacon, etc. This was being worked on at the time of my departure. (Later I learned that this was not accomplished because, following the many takeovers of industry leaders, the AMI was substantially downsized, eliminating and reducing many committees and projects.)

Obective 3

In preparing instructions for companies participating in the weekly reporting system, it became apparent that there were huge differences in cost accounting procedures, i.e., direct costs and indirect costs, methods for overhead allocation, etc. These differences affected final product costs, which in turn affected selling prices to the retail food stores. In many instances, it appeared that big differences in the shelf price for staple meat items like frankfurters were solely the result of different cost procedures. The committee therefore concluded that a "how to" seminar on cost accounting would be very helpful in bringing about a renaissance in the meat industry's cost accounting practices. The two- day seminar was held at the Palmer House in downtown Chicago and was very well received by several hundred attendees from all over the country. The program was complete with guest speakers, panels of industry experts, and a number of workshops for all the participants.

Objective 4

The accounting committee had a number of subcommittees, including one on data processing. This subcommittee's findings indicated that the general accounting departments and data processing departments were drifting apart and not marching along with the same drummer. Because of the success of the cost accounting seminar we went with a similar seminar on how to make the data processing department more effective. This seminar also proved to be a good one.

The reasons for these few paragraphs on my involvement with the American Meat Institute's accounting committee is to show that many nice side effects may result from participation in an industry trade association. In my case, I became good friends with many of the top players in the industry. It's a great advantage to pick up the phone and call your counterpart at one of your competitors and ask, "Bill, how are you handling . .?" Moreover, the interchange of ideas on common business matters was extremely helpful in broadening my business perspective. Finally, organizing and running those seminars was a great confidence builder, especially being able to sharpen my speaking skills by being at the mike on and off for the better part of two days.

The Minnow Swallows the Whale

There were considerable merger and takeover activities in the mid-sixties involving NYSE companies. Tender offers were common place, and it was relatively easy for aggressive corporate raiders to acquire a firm using no cash, only freshly printed preferred stock with whatever preference value and dividend rate was needed to make the transaction palatable to the seller and produce a net positive cash flow to the raider. Some of the takeover shams and abuses finally led to the adoption of Accounting Principles Board (APB) Numbers 16 & 17 in the seventies, covering Pooling of Interest and related accounting rules for acquisitions and mergers. This much-needed accounting requirement put an end to some senseless merger practices in the financial markets.

Throughout this period of mergermania and takeover activity, the markets continued to show little interest in the stocks of major meat packers. Despite their high, net book values and enormous annual sales, meat company stock prices languished at very low price earnings multiples. This was no surprise because historically meat industry earnings had been lackluster and erratic. Our country's agricultural programs and unpredictable weather had always been cited as reasons for the wide range of livestock prices and supplies, both of which severely impacted industry net income. Moreover, there was nothing to indicate that this was going to change. However, very suddenly in the mid-sixties there was an interest in meat company stocks. It was rumored that a confidential investment report on the industry had circulated on Wall Street pointing out the long-term potential of this undervalued group. The punch line of the report was the "What if, through better management, meat companies could increase their unit margin by a meager ½ cent per pound?" In Morrell's case, a ½ cent pound-margin increase on annual sales of 1.8 billion pounds would increase pretax income by $9 million, an amount exceeded only by the all-time pretax annual income record of $12.2 million in the 1959 fiscal year. At any rate, over the next few years nearly all of the big industry players were acquired and/or reorganized or restructured. If you look at a current NYSE listing you will not find Swift, Armour, Wilson, Morrell, Cudahy, Rath, or Oscar Mayer. The sole survivor was Hormel, which is still controlled by large blocks owned by the Hormel Foundation and employees.

The takeover of Morrell in 1967 was, of course, surprising and quick. It was carried out by AMK Corporation, a relatively small New York company that produced machinery for the rubber tire industry. AMK's stock was listed on the American Stock Exchange and was selling for about $9 per share. Their sales and net income for the most recent fiscal year were $31 million and $1.5 million respectively. They acquired approximately thirty-three percent of Morrell's stock through purchases on the open market. Morrell's stock price, about $27 per share, was depressed at the time because of poor earnings for its 1965 and 1966 fiscal years as well as the first half of the 1967 fiscal year. AMK's cash outlay for their stock purchase was a little under $10 million, an amount they had recently received for a parcel of land acquired by the government for highway purposes.

What happened to the stock prices of Morrell and AMK over the ensuing months was amazing. Each stock was frequently among the daily listing of the ten most active stocks, as well as the daily listing of new highs. Morrell stock soared to the sixty dollar range, undoubtedly Wall Street's anticipation that AMK would make a stock tender offer for the remaining two-thirds of Morrell shares that it did not own. Meanwhile, there was a lot of behind the scenes activity between the senior officers of both companies. AMK, of course, wanted immediate membership on the Morrell board, and began to flex its muscles a bit as a thirty-three percent owner is inclined to do. Mac, our CEO, had an excellent reason for not going along with a possible tender offer—there would be no business synergism whatsoever. And in terms of management skills, AMK's tiny staff had little to bring to the table. On the other hand Morrell had the financial muscle to adopt a number of strategies that could keep AMK at bay. If they succeeded would Morrell stock price fall back to the mid-twenties? Probably so, and I'm dead certain that stockholder value was the sole reason for not opposing the tender offer that was shortly made to Morrell stockholders. For each share of Morrell common the holder received:

½ share of AMK common		
(selling for 79 7/8 - 77 ½)	Value	$39.35
¼ share of AMK 3.20 Convertible Preferred		
(selling for 139.75)	Value	$34.85
	Total	$74.20

To no one's surprise, the stockholders of Morrell approved the merger plan. On December 31, 1967, Morrell's 140-year history came to an end. For the stockholders, it was a financial bonanza for a time because the AMK common shares soared to the $110 range. Shortly after reaching that peak, the stock started falling sharply and a few years later the market price was less than $10 a share.

Epitaph

Following the takeover, the changes in the corporate staff of Morrell were expected, and they were swift. The senior officers in charge of operations, marketing, and purchasing were the first to receive pink slips. They were gone without announcement or fanfare. A short time later Mac was relieved as CEO and was given an honorarium title of Assistant to the Chairman of the Board. Not surprisingly, my financial group was left intact because of the need to carry out two important corporate studies: (1) the establishment of a Corporate Grocery Products Division and (2) an in-depth analysis relating to the possible closing of the Ottumwa plant. These were massive and involved projects that I was deeply involved in for several months. Upon completion, the chairman, Eli Black, invited me to New York to discuss my reports as well as my moving to New York and future involvement with the new company. We spent most of the day together. When it was over I decided I didn't like the idea of moving, but more importantly, I knew for the long-term I could not work effectively with the new chairman. He was certainly intelligent, very quiet, serious, and a fine gentleman, and while our personalities were quite different, I knew we could get along all right. The problem was in the areas of business philosophies and strategies. We were on opposite sides on many important concepts, and I knew that these differences could never be reconciled. My future in business had reached a point where a watershed decision was at hand. That night on the plane back to Chicago I decided to resign from Morrell. As you will read in the beginning of the next chapter, it happened quickly, and in a few short weeks I was having a farewell luncheon with my great staff members. Leaving behind wonderful memories and camaraderie wasn't easy, but it had to be done. With the stroke of a pen, my thirteen years at Morrell faded in the sands of time.

Chapter 18

An Interesting Stint with the Pritzkers

This part of my business career began like a page out of an old, class-B movie or some of the recent subpar TV movie specials. To begin with, it was the kind of weather I hate—a bleak, rainy, overcast fall day with Chicago's famous wind blowing rain in my face as I walked from the commuter station across Chicago's Loop to Morrell's corporate office. The events of the previous day were still whirling in my head—the early morning flight to New York City, the long meeting with the chairman of the board, the midnight flight back to Chicago, and the long chat with my wife into the wee hours about my decision to resign from Morrell, and her usual 100% support. When I reached my office I saw my desk piled high with two days of mail; it was extra heavy because of the many special reports from our discussions in connection with the upcoming annual audit. After a brief update from my secretary, Ruth, about office matters of the previous day, I started digging into my mountain of mail. An hour or so later she buzzed me on the intercom and announced that a headhunter was on the line. I almost told her to say I wasn't in, but I always spoke briefly to reputable headhunters, so why change now? I asked Ruth to put him on the line. The man was from a small firm that I had never heard of. He was not calling about my staff needs in the financial and controller departments; he was calling me to see if I would be interested in a senior financial position for a prestigious Chicago firm. The position would be available in thirty days. I almost fell off my chair—it sounded too good to be true! Of course I expressed a keen interest and agreed to meet the client's personnel director the following day.

The interview was my first since leaving the University of Illinois campus twenty years earlier. The personnel director was a real class act—low key and laid back with a friendly and sincere personality that made the interview very pleasant, and most importantly, totally informative. When we finished, he knew me from A to Z and likewise, I knew his company from A to Z. It was the Marmon Group—just one of the many privately owned businesses of the Pritzker family of Chicago—one of the richest families in the United States. Despite their affluence, the Pritzkers maintained a very low profile and avoided publicity as much as possible. Therefore, it was not surprising that I had never heard of the company or the family name, even though the corporate offices were only two blocks up La Salle Street from Morrell's corporate office where I had spent the last thirteen years. The Marmon Group was a conglomerate of fifteen subsidiaries with annual sales approaching $100 million. The net income for the then current year was eight million—more than twice Morrell's best years on sales of almost one billion. The salary and related executive perks were excellent and the position of treasurer and its total responsibilities appeared very compatible with my skills and experience. The personnel director thought that the three senior executives would put their stamp of approval on me and that the last step was for me to meet each of them and then make my decision. Within a week or so I had had lengthy individual meetings with Bob Pritzker, CEO, and two other senior officers. Bob was my vintage and a fellow alumni from the University of Illinois. He was smart, honest, likeable, had a clever sense of humor, and above all, was a capable and practical business man. The other two officers were similar in makeup, and I was confident that the work environment would be comfortable, friendly, and much like that of a public company. I wanted to be sure that I wasn't getting involved with nepotism and the ugly spoils that are found in so many private companies.

Almost thirty days from the date of the call from the headhunter, I started with the Marmon Group as treasurer, replacing a veteran employee who had reached mandatory retirement age. I knew in advance that I would have the typical day-to-day responsibilities of the treasurer—cash management, insurance, taxes, pensions, credit, investments, etc. I also knew that the Marmon senior officers worked as a team on practically everything, and there might be considerable overlap in duties depending on the situation. In my case it meant being involved in mergers and acquisitions, backing up the corporate controller, and standing in the wings to play a key role in a future transaction. The organization of the Marmon Group could easily be a classic model for a lean and mean head office structure. Besides the CEO, there were four officers (controller, treasurer, legal, and personnel), two corporate accountants, and four secretaries. This staff of eleven people effectively directed fifteen companies throughout the United States and carried out extensive studies and investigations of possible acquisitions for continued corporate growth. The group was able to do this through a complete decentralized organization structure. Each subsidiary company was a separate entity. The president ran the company without any interference or meddling from the corporate office so long as it was on target with the annual budget. The budget, along with supporting schedules and explanations, was the foundation of the system—it was an absolute commitment. If the monthly numbers fell below budget for any reason, the CEO or another corporate officer wanted satisfactory explanations promptly. (Subsidiary presidents were well compensated, and if they didn't perform, they were replaced.) One of the keys in the organizational structure was the role of subsidiary controller—he did not report to the subsidiary president, but reported directly to the corporate office and in effect was the watchdog of the annual budget. This is the overview of the Marmon Group that I joined in 1968. In many ways it was not too different from Morrell in philosophy, style, and management.

Day-to-Day Treasurer Responsibilities

Cash Management
My thirteen years with Morrell were put to immediate use in cash management. Morrell employed several hundred salesmen throughout the forty-eight mainland states, each with a bank account, because the salesmen also made collections when they called on the customer. At the end of the workday, the salesmen would deposit the day's collections in a bank conveniently located near their residence. It was vital that these receipts flowed quickly and efficiently into the corporate cash pipeline for immediate use, because meat packing companies as a whole were never cash rich. My predecessor at the Marmon Group was no dummy, and he had orchestrated the cash movements satisfactorily by mostly feel and experience. However, it was possible and practical to systemize the entire system using more lock boxes, minimum bank balances, automatic transfers, and mailing procedures, which would speed up delivery—all of which would improve the receipt side of the cash equation. On the disbursement side of the cash equation, the cash position was improved by a specific schedule of when checks should be issued and mailed. The result was a system that had all cash working to the company's best advantage. The data obtained was monitored by my secretary by 10:00 AM each morning with a short phone call to each division

controller. With this information I could confidently proceed with the temporary investment of any surplus cash both as to amount and maturity.

Insurance

On the surface, the administration of a company's insurance program should not be terribly time consuming if the company's outside insurance brokers are a top organization, and the company's contact man (risk manager, treasurer, or whoever) has a good relationship with the insurance firm. Fortunately, this was exactly what I saw when I looked into my insurance responsibilities. The company had been placing all of its insurance through a Chicago division of Marsh & McLennan, one of the country's leading insurance firms, but more importantly, their account manager for the Marmon Group was Mr. Harold Hines, the most capable insurance man I ever met. (He later became senior vice president for Aon Corporation, one of the industry's largest firms, and was considered one of the great insurance brains when he died suddenly in the mid-eighties.)

After a review of all coverages and several meetings with Mr. Hines, I was totally satisfied that the insurance coverages were complete, at the right levels, and that the company procedures were effective in providing the necessary information flow to the insurance company. There was one obvious important factor that could not be accurately evaluated on a quick first review—namely, is the total bottom line cost for the coverages and related services by the insurance brokerage firms where it should be? I talked to the CEO about it, and it was a coincidence that he also thought the time might be ripe for a second opinion. The Marmon Group insurance account was a good one, and the company was continually receiving sales pitches from leading firms in this very competitive industry. He suggested a well-known firm that he was familiar with, and we went ahead with a complete insurance review by that firm. It was more time consuming than I thought but certainly the right thing to do from time to time. Upon completion, their findings confirmed the efficiency of our total program and cost thereof. No changes were made! Case closed.

Credit

Being a private company, it was not surprising that earnings per share was the company's second most important financial objective—cash flow was the first. Accordingly when I looked into credit procedures I found, again with no surprise, that every subsidiary was really on top of this function. My involvement with the subsidiary credit departments therefore was virtually nonexistent, other than to review and follow up the monthly reports and analysis of receivable billings and collections, aging schedules, and past-due balances. There was nothing in the procedures that needed change.

Taxes

The company's tax picture was relatively clean—a few acquisition issues were being contested by the IRS, and there were a few "sticky wickets" on some state tax issues in Michigan, but all of these did not add up to inordinate levels or demands. Shortly after I took over, the company's tax manager left for law school, and I quickly found a replacement with excellent credentials, and tax experience with a Fortune 500 concern. Together we revised the procedures for subsidiary tax reporting to the corporate office and also developed new working papers designed to expedite the preparation of both federal and state returns. While we were at all times concerned and mindful about tax planning, the major tax strategies were developed by Jay Pritzker, Chairman of the Board, and a real tax expert. In addition, Jay utilized two leading Chicago law firms from time to time on sophisticated tax issues. Quite obviously the tax function was efficiently organized and carried out. Like all tax work, it was tedious at times but a required way of life in today's business.

Pensions and Profit Sharing Plans

The company had several pension and profit sharing plans for certain salaried and hourly-paid employees. The funds were not material in amount and were administered by trust departments of several major banks. I received monthly reports from the trustees and held quarterly meetings to evaluate investment performance and related matters. This function was also working very satisfactorily and no changes were needed.

Investments

The company's chairman of the board and CEO decided the strategic acquisition plan for the company and likewise directed the kind and maturity of investments to be set aside for that purpose. As treasurer I had little involvement in the investment area other than to carry out their directions for the use of "excess cash."

Other Work Assignments

As expected, I received other responsibilities, and I was pleased that I was involved with them. As I mentioned earlier, the corporate officers all pitched in on an "as needed" basis on all kinds of corporate matters. My arrival coincided quite well with starting preparation for the company's annual report. Because I had a lot of experience on Morrell's annual reports, I "volunteered" for the assignment. The coordinating of the art work, layout, printing, photography, and financial data was just one of many interesting fill-in job responsibilities.

In top financial circles, the Pritzker name was known throughout the world. They had the financial muscle and brain power to undertake any kind of a deal. Since the mid-sixties they have acquired such publicized firms as Hyatt Hotels and Continental Air Lines. They have also grown the Marmon Group's annual sales to several billion dollars through an aggressive acquisition program. It was not surprising, therefore, for the company to be contacted almost daily by deal makers, business brokers, and business entrepreneurs seeking to sell their business. I'm sure many of these offers were immediately turned down, but those situations that had a good business purpose would get a hearing. It was almost a daily ritual to meet in Bob Pritzker's office to visit about a deal. Being a part of these meetings was a real experience. Bob had a relaxing and sincere manner and always kept the meetings on a friendly but businesslike basis. The meetings would usually last no more than an hour, and in that period Bob would conclude whether there was a conceptual interest requiring a follow-up work program on our part. Otherwise it would end on a friendly note, but in all instances it was an hour well-spent—we made a business friend, and we learned something that might help us in our existing business portfolios or in a future situation. All of the corporate officers who were available attended these meetings, and it was a representative example of the team approach on most corporate matters.

Some Pritzker Acquisition Rules

The company enjoyed a richly deserved reputation as being an astute deal maker. They didn't exactly use a prepared check list to make deals: they employed some common sense business principles too often overlooked. These are some of the important principles that I recall.

Keep it Simple
The company never wanted to become involved with businesses that were complicated and hard to understand. Moreover, there was little interest in marketing driven businesses that required high levels of sales promo-

tion and advertising that would also be subject to greater risk of obsolescence, competition, and consumer whims. This really narrowed the field to solid, grass roots, fundamental businesses with specialty niches that were well-established.

How about Cash Flow?

The company was just as interested in improving its earnings as public companies are, but being a private concern meant there was no market pressure. Because earnings forecasts at the acquisition table are usually inflated (no matter how many devil's advocates), the initial concern was cash flow. Could the company confidently expect a positive cash flow? If not, forget it!

What if and the Downside Risk

I often felt that Bob Pritzker invented the "Whaaaaat if?" It always took at least five seconds for him to say those two magical words, and then they would be followed with a lengthy list of potential disasters as bad or worse than some of Murphy's Laws. Very simply he wanted the bottom line on what might be, if the worst things possible happened to the prospective acquisition.

The First Loss Is the Smallest

Despite all of the painstaking care and investigations the company recognized that every deal would not prove to be a winner. Once in a while a deal would go sour. When that happened, the company simply would not hold onto it and continue to eat losses. It was disposed of as quickly and efficiently as possible.

These four observations are as timely and appropriate in the decade of the nineties as they were twenty-five years ago. It would be well to remember them as you wind through your business career.

The Annual Budget Review

The date of my joining the Marmon Group coincided perfectly with the program and schedule for the annual budget reviews to be made at the offices of all subsidiaries and divisions. I was pleased to be included on the corporate team that made the review. As noted earlier in this chapter, the Marmon Group's structure was about as decentralized as you could get in organizing a large group of companies, and the annual budget was an all-purpose commitment, a link and a control mechanism to the corporate office. The budget review itself was probably the most important day in the subsidiary's business year. Reviews were arranged in a sequence that would best accommodate the flight schedules of either commercial airlines or private charters that were used to reach outlying locations.

The reviews were very businesslike, but Bob Pritzker's easy manner kept them from getting too tense. The subsidiary personnel responded by not being overly nervous, and for the most part, made good presentations. The corporate office did not issue instructions requiring a specific agenda and the like; it was the responsibility of the subsidiary's CEO to present the coming year's operating plan and expected financial result in any manner he chose. Generally, he would start the review with a summary of past and present business highlights, that would serve as a frame of reference for the numbers developed for the coming year. As he proceeded through the budget he would call on members of his management team to elaborate on specific details—i.e., sales, plant operations, etc.

Throughout the presentations, members of the corporate team critiqued them very carefully. Bob Pritzker would chime in from time to time, but for the most part he remained relatively quiet, writing a few notes, and occasionally raising a question on a point overlooked by the corporate team. After all the presentations, he would summarize his impressions and give the CEO instructions on whatever budget revisions were required as a result of points raised by the corporate team. Then he would usually go through an exercise that I privately called "Bob Pritzker's Gallup Poll." He would select several relatively insignificant account balances in the operating ledger and ask to see a 100% backup for the budgeted amount. I remember one review where we looked at all the details on a local public relations account—$25 to sponsor a Little League baseball team, $15 for Girl Scout cookies, $50 for a Chamber of Commerce luncheon, etc. He was relentless in accounting for every item in the total. At first I wondered why. Then I realized it was a masterful bit of verifying the integrity of the entire budget, because if these small accounts were 100% documented, surely the company's staff was just as thorough on the major accounts. Moreover, it was another way of emphasizing a Marmon business principle, namely that all expenses should have a genuine business purpose irrespective of the amount.

These reviews took place almost twenty-five years ago at a time when most companies were just starting to think of budgets and profit plans.

Those companies that were into budgets were dealing with numbers that in the main were controller estimates. The budget numbers that we reviewed were the genuine articles—having been developed by the entire staff of the subsidiary from the ground up. They knew that the final budget was a commitment on which their performance would be judged. In today's world, strategic planning has become a way of life. It is a more disciplined and scientific methodology than the budget processes of twenty-five years ago. It frequently uses a lot of impressive buzz words and colored charts, but remember this—it's all meaningless if there are escape routes that can invalidate the all important doctrine of *commitment*.

The Private Company Difference

I had considerable experience with private companies before joining the Marmon Group—both as an auditor and a deal maker with Morrell. In my opinion, the typical public company tends to be different than the typical private company in their business philosophy and how they operate on a day-to-day basis.

Basic Business Philosophy
All public companies have two important common denominators. Much of the outstanding stock is owned by the public, and the company's board usually includes numerous outside directors. Accordingly, management tends to concentrate on creating stockholder value and operating the company in a way that is well perceived in financial circles.

By contrast, the private company is not under that kind of outside pressure. Of course they want to improve the value of the company, but they don't have to show an earnings increase in each quarter, and are quite willing to forego short-term profits for excellent long-term opportunities. Moreover, they don't have the additional pressure of cash dividends that public companies are constantly dealing with. These factors coupled with good management give the private company a distinct advantage over public companies and, in my opinion, explain the enormous success of such private companies as Johnson Wax and Hallmark Cards who are world leaders in their fields, as well as the Marmon Group whose annual sales are now in the billions. I remember a deal I handled that illustrates this advantage. It was a divestiture of a NYSE company because of a Federal Trade Commission ruling. The product line and the entire deal we were offered satisfied every Marmon criteria by a wide margin. In the final week of fine tuning the purchase agreement, I was able to negotiate major contract points that decreased our downside risk even further. Because of existing sales contracts, a satisfactory profit for Marmon was assured for three years, even after allowing for a possible 100% write-off of the seller's properties. Several days before the purchase agreement was to be signed, the prime interest rate jumped a half point. Shortly after the announcement, Bob Pritzker came into my office and said, "Lloyd, I'm calling off the deal. I know we are sure of a nice profit for three years, but after that who knows? The product fits fine, but I'm not thrilled about it. Furthermore, with the prime rate increase announced this morning, I think it is a signal for us to wait awhile. We can probably put our cash to better use." Just like he said, the deal was called off, and later in the year the cash was used to make a far better acquisition. This last minute cancellation would never have happened in a public company. By that time the deal would have been approved by the company's board, and the CEO would have looked like an idiot calling a special meeting to cancel the deal because of an increase in the prime interest rate.

The Marmon Group conducted its businesses on the same high ethical level as Morrell and the other large public companies I had experience with. In every way, Marmon's policies were compatible with first-rate public companies. The working atmosphere at Marmon was always very pleasant, and there was no nepotism or any double standards to contend with. I bring this up, however, as a warning that all private companies are not like the Marmon Group. During my career I saw too many of them run by owners who surrounded themselves with overpaid and underqualified relatives. In addition, they usually raided the company bank accounts to buy airplanes, yachts, and vacation homes they acquired for personal use. This kind of a company is headed for extinction, and if you unfortunately become employed with such a company, don't be overly misled by the glamour of a corporate jet. Leave it, as soon as you can make an acceptable job change.

****

As the end of my first year with the Marmon Group came to a close, I could see some dark clouds developing over my job as treasurer. On paper there was an impressive list of responsibilities, but in reality they were not terribly challenging. Fortunately, the special corporate duties that I was involved in—the annual report and mergers and acquisitions were challenging and satisfying, but there wasn't enough of these for me. I had been hired to be involved in two important projects that had both been cancelled. Having spent thirteen years at Morrell working at a pace of 100 miles an hour, it was a killing adjustment to throttle down to a slower work pace of 8:30 to 5:00, five days a week. I could count the number of times I called my wife to tell her I would not be taking the 5:25 train to Glenview on one hand. One night when she picked me up at the train station, I must have looked very gloomy to her because she asked if something was wrong at work. "You're not yourself, lately," she said. That was it? My wife's perception confirmed what had started to gnaw inside of me. The dark cloud suddenly turned pitch black. It was time to talk to Bob Pritzker.

Bob was very understanding and made the same observations as my wife. He cited a number of excellent financial posts in different Pritzker organizations that I might consider. They were attractive except for one thing: they either required moving out of Chicago, or staying in Chicago and facing frequent travel on a Monday to Friday basis. "Look them over," he said, "and take whatever time you need to make a decision."

Several months later I was in Bob's office saying goodbye. I left on very friendly terms that still exist today.

Chapter 19

The Consultant—Working on Center Stage

Most of the important things in my life did not result from any kind of careful planning. My plans usually followed Robert Burns's classic observation about plans—they generally ended up in the wastebasket. Getting into the consulting business was typical. It was a combination of pure-chance, accidents and serendipities.

Making a career change at age forty-seven can be sobering and soul searching. It can also be rewarding. In my case I took a long, objective look at myself, my personal life, and my business credentials. I saw a healthy guy with a wonderful wife and children, a great circle of friends, and a very satisfying lifestyle. On top of that, good money management and successful investing had produced a strong family balance sheet. On paper my business background and experience were very good, but there was a definite weakness—practically all of it was in the meat packing industry, which was in the throes of suffering a quick death. Putting everything on the scale, I concluded that our family life in the Chicago area was too good, and I didn't want to jeopardize it. I then advised Bob Pritzker that I was not interested in any of the opportunities he had offered me, and I also advised several corporate recruiting firms that I was not interested in any senior financial positions out of the Chicago area. I had made up my mind—I was going to open an office and establish a CPA and financial advisory practice in the Chicago area. I had the contacts, reputation, skills, and finances needed to make this venture a success. I planned to start right after the Christmas holidays in 1970.

Over the holidays I ran into Wally McCallum, my old boss at Morrell. We had not seen each other for over a year, and so we got together for lunch to bring each other up-to-date. I told him about my plans, and he almost jumped out of his chair. "Wait until you hear what I've been doing.

I started a financial practice a few months ago, and I have so much business I don't know where to turn!" He went on to describe that he had a half dozen NYSE companies on monthly retainers and several outstanding private companies wanting him to handle the sale of their respective companies. Would I like to come on board and be his partner? This came right out of the blue, and I wasn't prepared for a blockbuster question like that. I agreed to give it some real thought and meet with him in a few days. At that meeting we got into the nuts and bolts of the business. It was very interesting, and from a financial point of view, very promising. It wasn't exactly my original plan, but it was reasonably close to it. We shook hands, and in a few days I was starting out on a new course in the financial world.

Our offices were in a new building located on Chicago's Magnificent Mile on Michigan Avenue and were handsomely appointed. We prepared a small brochure that provided our business background as well as the specific kind of consulting work we would undertake—namely corporate growth and development, mergers, acquisitions, and divestitures, primarily in the food, meat, and related industries. We had no interest in being an all-purpose management consulting firm and trying to compete with the national organizations or the hundreds of small consulting firms in the Chicago area.

Most consulting engagements are made on the basis of reputation earned through known performance, and through credibility and friendships developed through extensive business relationships. Wally McCallum's performance at Morrell of growing annual sales from 300 million to over a billion was a feature story in *Fortune*, and the Morrell-AMK merger in the prior year was one of the hottest deals that had captured Wall Street's attention. I did not have that kind of national notoriety, but I was well known in the meat industry. As part of my responsibilities as chairman of the industry's accounting committee, I conducted numerous seminars. And as part of my executive responsibilities at Morrell, I "quarterbacked" nearly every acquisition during the growth years. The early seventies were a booming period for mergers and acquisitions. Our timing for this partnership could not have been better.

One of the most important but underrated positions in a business organization is the administrative assistant to the head man. That position is even more important in a small professional group that is dealing primarily with high level clientele. In addition to the normal skills required of an executive secretary, that person needs extra measures of finesse, writing and communication skills, common sense, and above all the right level of alter ego when the boss is not present. Wally McCallum's administrative assistant at Morrell had been a private secretary for two prominent men— one became a U.S. Senator and the other, a member of the President's Cabinet. She came on board and fit in perfectly, becoming a significant contributor to the success of the partnership.

Wally and I were no strangers to the consulting field. Both of us had experience as accounting consultants at Price Waterhouse during the early part of our careers, and in our later years as corporate executives, we had extensive experience with a host of big national consulting organizations, as well as smaller specialty firms. In short, we had worked both sides of the street and knew the mind-set and inter-workings of the consultant in the relationship with the clientele. Although no two engagements were exactly the same, our work could be classified as follows.

Acquisition Searches

Typically, a company seeking acquisitions does not want to advertise its goals. It prefers to have much of the preliminary contact and screening done by an outside organization on a hush-hush basis. This was the case even with large companies that had their own acquisitions department. We would supplement their work and act as devil's advocates on searching and screening, but handle the contacts and the preliminary legwork before disclosing the client's identity and getting our client's CEO involved. In this way, leaks were minimized and much executive time was saved. As deals progressed toward fruition, we remained very active as advisors and assistants in all phases of the transaction—the contract preparation, financing arrangements, negotiation of the purchase price, etc.

Sales of Private Companies

The typical private company rarely has the personnel to efficiently orchestrate the sale of the company. Moreover, the owners are frequently "married" to the business and have an unrealistic idea of its value. Further, there is the problem of sentiment, and concern over what will happen to the company's loyal employees—their job titles, salaries, perks, etc. It is this kind of company that we often accepted as a client. Our role was to start at the very beginning and assist the company in preparing for the sale. Among other things, we prepared a seller's historical financial prospectus, developed a realistic range of the company's value in the market, and arranged the contract "mechanics" (sale of the company for cash? notes? tax-free exchange of stock?) to achieve the best financial result, tax-wise, for the company's owners. Finally, we anticipated possible problems related to employees' total compensation and future job responsibilities and worked out acceptable solutions. In summary, we orchestrated the transaction from beginning to end, keeping it confidential at all times. With thorough planning and client cooperation, news of the possible sale of the company was not leaked to the public. This is not always possible because sometimes along the way somebody talks. The impact on the company when this happens can be quite disruptive. Fortunately, we did not experience any major leaks in any of our engagements.

Special Assignments for the CEO
Enormous changes were taking place in the meat and food industries, and we accepted a variety of assignments from CEOs in those fields as well as acquisitions, sales, and divestitures. These included matters pertaining to strategic planning, product profitability, personnel, and management systems.

There is a definite need for consultants in today's competitive and high-tech business environment, otherwise there would not be so many. There are many good ones, but sadly, far too many marginal and incompetent firms whose activities are tantamount to hustling. Why is this? First of all, any Tom, Dick, and Harry can hang out shingle and call the firm a consulting group. Secondly, there is virtually no regulatory controls or professional standards or requirements to establish a consulting business. We were very cognizant of the unsavory stigma associated with a segment of this business, and accordingly adopted our own "golden rules."

1) Never solicit or promote business
2) Never accept an engagement from a firm you don't like
3) Never accept an engagement unless you are totally confidant that you will do a superior job.

We never wavered from these principles, and they were undoubtedly a contributing factor to the firm's success.

It is pretty obvious from the above captions that our clientele and engagements were quite varied, challenging, and interesting. Our work took us to a number of board rooms, Wall Street, and other financial centers. Indeed, we were on stage a great deal of the time being observed like we were in a fish bowl. That's the way it should be. Our fees were not cheap, and our clients were entitled to view a professional performance. These successes somehow found a way of getting in the grapevine that spread important news to the pervasive financial community. The following paragraph is an example of this.

The client was a respected company in the meat industry. Its annual sales were in excess of $100 million, but its net income had been dismal for a number of years. The family had engaged a number of prominent organizations to sell the business, but without success. Because of our reputation, they came to us for advice. We carefully looked the company over and concluded that the situation was not hopeless. The company had proved that it could sell its products, but it simply didn't know how to sell them profitably. That's easy to say but hard to do in the very competitive meat business. We believed we could help them achieve a dramatic turnaround, and we accepted the assignment. We made ongoing studies and recommendations for all phases of the business, which were reviewed weekly with management for implementation. In a little over a year the company was operating consistently at a satisfactory profit level, and we were able to sell the company for cash at a price greater than book value—a number beyond the owner's wildest dreams of a year ago. Investment banking groups and other financial organizations frequently publish a "Tombstone" ad in *The Wall Street Journal* of a significant sale or merger and their role in the transaction. We chose not to do this, but nevertheless we had calls from all parts of the country within a few days about the deal.

In life, success breeds success. In the consulting business success *definitely* breeds success. This deal not only helped bring in more business, but it helped me out individually. I was invited to go on the board of Woodhead Industries, Inc., an excellent public company in the electrical industry, as well as several other boards of private companies in the Chicago area.

****

The business rolled along nicely for about five years without any problems. We continued to maintain a fine client base, enjoy the work, and achieve a very satisfactory level of annual net income, but we reached a point where it was best to split up and go our separate ways. Wally was now in his early seventies, and while in good health, simply had too many other demands on his time. In my case, the time was right for me to establish my own identity in the financial community. We worked out a very agreeable and logical arrangement. Wally would continue working with the big NYSE companies at his own pace and his own time and involvement. I would continue with the smaller Chicago area firms, which I was handling. We would maintain our regular offices, and in a pinch we could help each other out if needed.

The experiences of those five years would be a perfect parody for Bob Hope's timeless "Thanks for the memories." A fun chapter of my business career had ended—life goes on. After a very cordial lunch, handshake, and "Godspeed," I was eager to leave and finally start "Lloyd Kurkowski & Co."

Chapter 20

Welcome to Lloyd's of London

One of the great satisfactions from my consulting practice was the realization that the learning process in the financial world can continue unabated even after thirty years away from college academia. It was a revelation that there were so many common denominators and similarities in business. While individual businesses had some idiosyncrasies and different operating practices, they all had a common need for:

1) Financial controls
2) Product line profitability
3) Strategic planning knowhow
4) A timely and accurate management information system

In my consulting role, my niche was like an outside CFO working a day or two a month with presidents and CEOs of small- and medium-sized businesses. I had clients in a number of businesses—machine tool, plastic packaging, retail displays, pizza, children's toys, restaurant supply, and others. I never turned away a prospective client solely on the basis of what business they were in. I always felt that I could catch on, and if I couldn't do a top-notch job, I never sent them a bill.

Referrals from banks, law firms, and other professional organizations were the sources of most of my clients. From time to time I would take on a client as an accommodation to a personal friend. That's exactly how I became involved in the insurance industry, as well as an unusual chapter in my financial career. The business was a start-up insurance company that administered medical and hospitalization policies. They carried out the marketing, claims paying, and all the functions of an insurance company except that it was not at risk. That was the responsibility of a large U.S.

insurance company and Lloyd's of London, the worldwide insurance giant, which was just getting into underwriting health insurance in the United States. The two big insurance firms paid the administrator a fee for its services; this income, along with the interest on premium trust fund investments combined to make the total revenue base for the administrator.

The organizer of the company and 100% stockholder was a very personable, good looking insurance industry veteran in his late thirties. He had a keen and creative insurance mind and was quick to see opportunities in imaginative new products. Medical and hospital costs were increasing at double-digit annual rates and expense minded insurance and senior executives were very responsive to approaches that could at least contain the escalation of these costs. He addressed this problem in a number of ways. First of all he was very selective in the marketing of the policies emphasizing companies that historically had better medical claim-loss ratios. Moreover, he emphasized marketing to companies that had a more favorable employee census age wise. (Obviously, firms with younger employees tend to have fewer claims than firms with older employees.) Secondly, he organized a very efficient claims department—one that "turned around" quickly. (Turn around is industry jargon for processing the claim upon receipt and then sending the claim check promptly to the employee.) The claims department employees were pros who had the experience to spot padded expenses and many other irregularities that were prevalent in the health care practice. All these factors added up to an insurance program that was very attractive in the marketplace. In fact, that was their problem. The level of business far exceeded their expectations, and their primitive systems could not handle the workload. The CEO had not seen a financial statement in four months, bank accounts had not been reconciled, all subsidiary ledgers were woefully out of balance, and worse yet, important reports of premium and claim activity for the underwriters were past due. I started to have second thoughts about this assignment because it was not compatible with my normal practice. Moreover, I didn't have the staff needed to do the work. I really felt sorry for the owner who had worked so hard to get a great business started successfully, and was now on the verge of losing it because of the poor advice and work by a small inexperienced accounting firm who threw up their hands and abandoned ship. I let my heart rule my head and agreed to bring the records up-to-date and install a new system. I coaxed a few old buddies (top professionals) to come out of early retirement, and after several weeks and some midnight oil burning, our mission was accomplished. We instructed the employees on working the new system, and they loved it. We went over the up-to-date financial statements with the owner, and we also reviewed projected profits and a number of financial strategies. He was jubilant, to say the least, and amazed at the profit level for so young a business. At the end of our meeting he asked me if I could meet him for lunch at my convenience—he wanted to talk about how I might play a role in the company's future.

A few days later we met at the plush Metropolitan Club in the Sears Tower. He outlined a surprising and very interesting proposal offering me to

1) become a director of his company;
2) take over as president of the company after phasing out my consulting practice (He would be chairman of the board and work exclusively on developing new insurance products);
3) acquire a twenty percent interest in the company for $1.00.

This was indeed an attractive offer. For one thing, the idea of running a company, although initially on the small side, was very appealing because I felt that I had acquired the overall skills needed to be a good company president or CEO. Moreover, I could see enormous growth, and I was certain that the company would not be a small one very long. The financial package was excellent—fine salary, club memberships, a car, and other usual perks. But the real plum was a substantial share of the company's annual profits. For the longer term, say five to seven years, I could easily see my twenty percent stock interest being worth seven figures. The medical and hospitalization insurance market was virgin territory for self-insurance. The company had a jump start on getting into the field because it not only had the organization, but it also had the contacts and acceptance with Lloyd's of London who would provide the excess coverages for stop losses.

I was once again in one of those soul-searching evaluations of what to do. I had been in the consulting field for over six years; I enjoyed the work and the freedom of being my own boss, as well as a very nice annual income. Should I give this up because the grass was greener in the insurance offer? Running this promising insurance company really appealed to me, and after much deliberation I decided that I would accept the offer if I could (1) maintain an ongoing relationship with my important clients and (2) spend more time with the owner and confirm that the human chemistry between us was okay. This was agreeable to the owner, and in a few days we were on a week-long golf holiday in Pinehurst, North Carolina, with our wives. It was a wonderful week, and my wife and I both agreed that the owner and his wife were top-notch, sincere, and nice intelligent human beings.

The purpose of this rather detailed story about this part of my career is to point out the importance of checking all the bases when making a job change—particularly later in your career when the opportunities may not be as plentiful. I felt that I had turned over every stone and considered all possibilities in making this change, but as you will read in the next few paragraphs, you never know what might come out of the closet.

For a little more than a year all phases of the business performed very well. Our trip to London to meet the underwriters at Lloyd's was exciting and productive. They liked the profit rate we returned to their respective names and assured us of a continuing relationship not only for the present policy, but also for the self-insurance product that we were developing. The chairman in his role as a developer of new insurance products, organized a company specializing in excess surplus lines that was successful from day one. We owned sixty percent of the stock and provided all of the initial financing. The remaining forty percent was held by two insurance veterans who were also the key employees running the day-to-day operations.

Our regular insurance product continued to show very good growth: our basic systems performed very effectively and employee morale was high. From my own standpoint, I was quite satisfied with my new role and was excited about the company's potential with the self-insurance program. I was also pleased that I was able to maintain continuing relationships with all of my old important consulting clients by using breakfast and lunch meetings here and there and on a few weekends.

The company's rosy picture, however, did not last too long. Despite a very high salary, our chairman's newly acquired penchant for the good life went out of control. Suddenly he was driving a top of the line foreign automobile, taking off on long vacations via air charters and first class airline fares, and, in general, conducting his private life like a big shot millionaire, when in fact he had very little personal net worth. This lifestyle was financed by very hefty interest-free advances from the company. The company's cash flow was already paying out sizeable sums for its plush offices in the Sears Tower as well as a swank lake front penthouse that the company rented for visiting firemen. It was impossible for me to curtail an eighty percent owner, particularly when the business was doing well and the cash was available. This all changed quite suddenly when a political change caused us to lose our largest account, one that brought about forty percent of the company's revenue. At that point we went on a lean and mean program to cut expenses and intensify our selling efforts to make up for the severe impact of losing our largest account. I made it quite clear to the owner that he had to curtail his spending activities like everyone else, and he agreed to do so. However, it wasn't long before an even bigger problem started to emerge. It was a nonaccounting problem to be sure, and it is a real killer in the nineties: Alcohol, Alcohol, Alcohol.

I am not a nondrinker. I enjoy a scotch and soda before dinner, and a glass of good wine with dinner. But throughout my business career, I followed the practice of alcohol-free lunches, relenting on a handful of occasions when having a bottle of beer with the client or the birthday guest was the right thing to do. The chairman and I did not have lunch together very often. There wasn't any need to. Each of us used lunch as a meeting place with customers and associates important to the company. When the chairman and I did have lunch, he would order his favorite drink, Bombay Martini on the rocks. Once in a while he would have a second one, and I would razz him about falling asleep when he returned to the office. I didn't think he had any problem with the bottle, but some telltale signs started to appear—the lunches got longer, and he seemed to avoid me after returning from lunch. When I popped into his office I could smell the combination of gin and mouth spray on his breath. But the real proof came by accident when his favorite restaurant inadvertently included the drink tickets with their monthly statement that always came directly to me. There it was, enough Bombay Martinis each day to make President Carter's "three-martini lunch" obsolete and inadequate. How about six or seven? I did not sit idly. I promptly had a very long talk with him about his drinking. I had seen him advance from a social drinker to a heavy drinker and now a most certain alcoholic. I had seen this wonderful, likeable, intelligent man gradually develop a drunkard's mean streak as well as terribly irrational and egotistical outbursts. He promised to cut down, and God love him, he tried. As the months passed, the situation became worse and, of course, the impact on the business was devastating. The culmination of his drinking problems surfaced when we went to London to renew our self-insurance proposal with Lloyd's underwriters. He was so inadequately prepared that he gave them a flim-flam excuse for not presenting it at the time, and said he would be back in a few months after we had crossed every 't' and dotted every 'i'. (This was pure baloney.) When we returned to our home office there was another of his "no brainers" to unscramble. Upon his order alone, delivery of hardware had been made to our office as part of a complete computer installation—something that we had planned to do about a year later.

I had been foolish enough to think that my patience and counseling would curb his problem. He needed professional help, but would not admit it or even consider it. Despite this, I knew that the company could overcome his alcoholism and be very successful, thanks to a talented organization, a solid management system, and a self-insurance product that would soon be an enormous profitmaker. Although my twenty percent stock interest could have potentially been worth seven figures in a few years, job happiness and an ulcer-free body were more important; I decided to resign. We agreed on a financial settlement for my stock interest that because of tax purposes, I elected to receive on a deferred basis over five years.

What happened after I left is a good news/bad news story. First the good news. The self-insurance program was finally put together and it was immediately a huge success. The company's annual net income went through the roof, and it soon earned a prominent reputation in its field. So much so that it was receiving lucrative merger offers from a big industry player.

Now the bad news. The owner finally admitted his problem and checked into a treatment center. It helped, but he never conquered his problem. Along the way he acquired another awful habit—sports gambling. The company's enormous profits and cash levels were just too tempting for him. When it was over, all of the company's cash and premium trust funds had flowed into the gambler's coffers, and in doing so, he broke a number of federal laws. He was indicted by the U.S. District Attorney and pleaded guilty to taking $1,400,000 of premium trust funds for his own use. He was sentenced to a three-year term in a white collar prison. The company was liquidated and went out of business.

I personally felt terrible about the finale to this segment of my career. This likeable, robust friend was ninety-nine percent as fine as anyone I've ever known or worked with, but his one percent weakness, which is in all of us, simply devoured him. From a business point of view, however, it was a profitable experience because I learned a lot about the insurance business, and I also enhanced my management skills considerably. Financially speaking it was very satisfactory in more ways than one. Because of my having seen and worked with Lloyd's of London, I saw this worldwide insurance citadel as an excellent profit opportunity and became a member (more commonly called a "name") in 1979. I continued as a member for ten years, receiving a nice check every year for my share of the profits. When I reached the "65" mark and retired from business, I also resigned from Lloyd's: (1) I didn't need the income, so why be exposed to possible losses that might topple my retirement nest egg and (2) I saw some ominous signals that I thought might spell trouble ahead for the insurance in-dustry—i.e., the enormous scope of losses related to asbestos, Environ-mental Protection Agency (EPA) regulations, and medical malpractice, as well as the incredible escalation in damages awarded in personal injury lawsuits. My perception happened to be right, and starting in 1989 Lloyd's was hit with a sharp downturn in annual results that sent shockwaves throughout the financial markets of the world. In the United States the Lloyd's downturn hit the front pages a great deal because U.S. names were among those incurring heavy losses.

Because of the importance of Lloyd's in the global financial world, the overhauling of its infrastructure, which is currently going on, coupled with the fact that Lloyd's literally wrote the book on the insurance business, I believe it is necessary to embellish this book with a brief history about Lloyd's, and how it operates.

The Lloyd's of London History

Coffee houses in London were the primary meeting place for merchants and shipmasters during the latter part of the seventeenth century. It was in those houses where merchants with ships and cargoes would meet with brokers and underwriters to place marine insurance with men of wealth and integrity who were prepared to meet their share of any claim by put-ting their personal fortunes at risk. In 1687, Edward Lloyd founded a cof-fee house in London, and although Mr. Lloyd did not underwrite any insur-ance, he was quick to recognize that the most important prerequisite for successful insurance was accurate and up-to-date information. He promptly set up a network of ports throughout Britain and the continent that could provide all the significant news of shipping movements which he then of-fered to his clientele. He also organized the auction of ships and equipment and later, published a regular bulletin, "Lloyd's News." His coffee house rapidly became the leading center for merchants, shipmasters, and marine underwriters and literally was indispensable to anyone writing risks on the high seas. Edward Lloyd died in 1713 but the coffee house activities were carried on by his heirs adinfinitum. It continued to grow in size and impor-tance, along with his clientele whose insurance activities also grew by leaps and bounds as London became one of the world's leading maritime cen-ters. Through the years the house was moved to larger facilities a number of times and along the way simplified its name to just "Lloyd's." The most recent Lloyd's office building opened in 1986. It is a very modern skyscraper and one of the tallest and largest in London's financial district. From these simple beginnings the underwriters at Lloyd's, who originally specialized in only marine risks, ultimately expanded their skills to any and all types of risk taking. In this connection, Lloyd's frequently makes newspaper headlines when it issues such policies as those on Betty Grable's legs (World War II's most famous pinup girl) or the throwing arms of leading NFL Quarterbacks.

In its early coffee house days, the underwriters at Lloyd's were largely individual free-lancers, but over time this changed to a more organized club-like structure requiring membership fees, rules of conduct, and financial guarantees. Because of Lloyd's prestige and track record its activities were exempt from many regulatory controls until 1871 when it became a corporation by an Act of Parliament with its affairs governed by a committee elected from among its members. At about this time, the majority of Lloyd's members joined together to underwrite large risks, and the syndicate system evolved with members participating in more than one syndicate. This original act has been amended a number of times, the most recent in 1982.

Present Day Structure and Overview

The corporation of Lloyd's is responsible for providing the marketplace and facilities as well as assisting its council and committee on policy making and administration. As separate entities, the corporation, its council and committee does not and cannot underwrite any insurance business—that is done solely by the approximately 350 underwriting syndicates. The corporation's income is derived from noninsurance activities such as membership fees, rental and investment income etc. Its current balance sheet shows net assets of about 300 million pounds sterling consisting principally of fixed assets and current investments. There are approximately 150 managing insurance agencies, each of which manages a number of syndicates. Each syndicate consists of a number of names, and in all of Lloyd's there are approximately 350 syndicates and upwards of 26,000 names from around the world (20,000 from the United Kingdom and several thousand from the U.S.) which provide the financial backing for all of Lloyd's underwriting. At the present time total annual premium income of all insurance underwriting at Lloyd's is approximately seven billion pounds sterling. (At current exchange rates it's about eleven billion in U.S. dollars.)

Becoming a name at Lloyd's is somewhat like joining a country club. You must be sponsored by an underwriting agent and must exceed some fairly high financial thresholds in terms of personal liquid assets and total assets, as well as a hefty level of annual net income. After official admission as a member, each name must deposit securities or a letter of credit equal to 30% of the premiums that he agrees to underwrite. In my case, I authorized a premium limit of 450,000 pounds in my last year as a member and accordingly arranged for my Chicago bank to issue a letter of credit in favor of Lloyd's in the amount of 150,000 pounds. This was the backup or reserve in the event that my participating syndicates experienced a loss year. In the case of a loss year, a "cash call" is first issued to the respective names, and if not paid by the date due, the managing Lloyd's agent draws upon the letter of credit for the name's pro rata share of the loss. A further level of financial backup is the Lloyd's Central Fund whose assets are in the billions and will take care of insured's claims if the syndicate member's deposits are insufficient.

I was sponsored by R.W. Sturge & Co., an extremely successful agency that managed fifteen syndicates in very diverse and selective underwritings—marine, aviation, motor, and nonmarine, which encompassed many categories of risk taking. The Sturge Company had a wonderful track record of profitable performance; when I joined Lloyd's in 1979 it had recorded only one loss year in its long history, and during my ten-year membership, I continued to receive a nice check every year for my share of the net income.

There is major misconception about Lloyd's that I would like to clear up and that is the matter of a name's investment in Lloyd's. Presently, the membership initiation fee is 3,000 pounds and that's it—no annual dues thereafter. Other than this, there is no real investment in Lloyd's because the securities deposited with Lloyd's or with the bank issuing the letter of credit to Lloyd's, continue to be registered in the name of the member who continues to receive all of the dividends and/or interest income on such securities.

There is one final requirement that is a hallmark in becoming a name at Lloyd's. You must meet with the council in Lloyd's historic Captain's Room in London that is replete with memorabilia of Lord Nelson's and other British naval triumphs on the high seas. After a cordial conversation, the council members will explain in complete detail (several times) the principle of *Unlimited liability* and whether the applicant fully understands it. When the applicant finally says "I do," they sign the official documents, pay their admission fee, and become a name.

Welcome to the Club

Becoming a name at Lloyd's is a little scary to say the least. To begin, the insurance business is very complex and a distinct two-dimensional business. First, you have the underwriting and/or risk taking side with its long history of unpredictability, ups and downs, and many surprises. Second, you have the investment side where premiums are deposited in trust funds but invested until funds are needed to pay claims of policy holders. With current, wide fluctuations in interest rates, that integral part of the business is likewise somewhat unpredictable. A second complication arises because the underwriting business for a given year is not closed until the end of the final year of the policy, at which time the gain or loss is determined. (Example: the gain or loss on all policies issued in calendar year 1988 would be determined at the close of business, December 31, 1990, and assuming a net profit, around June 15, 1991, the name would receive their check applicable to the 1988 year.) I know it's pretty confusing, but sit tight. There is one more hurdle to cross. For tax purposes, the basis for reporting income is a mixture of cash and accrual basis accounting, and although there is a tax treaty between the Inland Revenue of the UK and the Internal Revenue Service of the U.S., the rules have been so tricky that even sharp U.S. tax experts in England and the United States struggle with all the tax ramifications of the treaty. Accordingly, I am sure that most names get professional tax advice on all Lloyd's related matters.

United States names who own stock in public companies are accustomed to receiving quarterly reports on how their companies are doing. That is not the case for most syndicates at Lloyd's. Until several years ago there simply was no interim financial reports of any kind and a name would be totally in the dark for a solid year until the time of the annual meeting with the principals of their managing agency. At that meeting they would receive an income check (or a debit memo for a loss year), a brief explanation about the operations for the year, and an announcement as to when the name's tax report and the agency's audited statements would be mailed. This was obviously not the best way to run the railroad, and while some of this inadequacy of informal reporting could be partially explained by the complexity of the operations, the more likely explanation is, "We've not done it before."

The foregoing paragraphs under this caption fairly summarizes the Lloyd's that I saw in my ten years ending in 1988. It was humming along pretty well, turning a nice profit every year and growing in capacity and annual premiums. Nevertheless there were little tremors here and there indicating it was time to take a fresh look at the full spectrum of Lloyd's operation. In early 1991 a task force was formed including top financial and insurance minds of Lloyd's as well as highly respected outside experts. Their mission: prepare a route forward for the next century.

What's Ahead at Lloyd's

The total operation at Lloyd's up to 1989 was probably a perfect example of the phrase, "If it ain't broke—don't fix it." But the wave of severe losses in 1989, 1990, and 1991 due to hurricanes, earthquakes, and a greater incidence of nonrecurring events such as the Lockerbie, Scotland B-747 terrorist bombing loss was certainly a factor behind the creation of a task force to examine where Lloyd's is, where it should be going, and how.

The task force report was completed in January 1992 and is still undergoing considerable evaluation. The 235-page report addresses many issues. Some of the more important ones are:

1) Reaffirming Lloyd's position as a world leader in the nonlife insurance industry. Retaining its unique structure of names, syndicates, and managing agents. Using this pool of talent and Lloyd's reputation along with building stronger and more effective distribution channels will insure its future success.

2) Strengthening Lloyd's capital base to accommodate the need for growth. This would include strengthening the names' rights, improved financial information, a high-level central stop-loss cover for names while preserving some of the principles of unlimited liability. Also access to corporate capital would be permitted under certain conditions as well as admission of corporate members on a limited liability basis.

3) Improving Lloyd's competitiveness through market wide cost reduction, syndicate expense reductions through consolidations, etc.

4) Creating a Lloyd's Market Board that can be responsible for business strategy and will assume the responsibility of business issues currently handled by the council and committee. The proposal is so organized that all these functions can be supervised quickly and effectively.

The Task Force report has been well-received and currently is in various stages of fine tuning and implementation. The new and restructured Lloyd's that you may be dealing with at some time in your career should continue to be a world insurance leader, financially strong, and with a rich history of underwriting expertise.

Chapter 21

Back to the Ledgers for the Last Hurrah

My swan song to the insurance company was just a few days away from my 55th birthday. While that's a relatively young age, a number of my successful classmates from the University of Illinois were already enjoying early retirement. That was the last thing on my mind—the first thing was a well-deserved vacation following my traumatic departure from the insurance company. Shortly after this incident, my wife and I were on a flight to San Francisco for two weeks of golf, good restaurants, and sight-seeing. This was followed by two more weeks of R&R with the children in the beautiful North Woods of Wisconsin. After a glorious month, I was ready to resume my consulting practice. I set up shop in the offices of Wally McCallum, my longtime business associate and former partner. I had several regular clients, two directorships with private companies, a directorship with Daniel Woodhead, Inc., as well as a large number of open-end arrangements for mergers, acquisitions, and deal making. Within a couple of weeks I was happily back in the groove with a very nice routine. I was confident that this latest consulting mode would be my last hurrah. Wrong!! Six months later I received a call from Woodhead's CEO. "Could you meet me at the Club for lunch today?" I was sure it wasn't for golf because it was a very rainy, chilly day. I was right. He wanted to tell me that the company's CFO had resigned and moved back to his hometown where he had acquired a manufacturing concern in the building supply business. "Woodhead needs a top CFO." He went on to say half-jokingly, "Would you like to leave that soft consulting job and go back to work? You know, of course, we'll make it worth your while." I assured him that I would consider the offer very carefully and let him know within a week.

After working in the financial world for thirty years, I had developed my own criteria for what constitutes a good job. Intellectual challenge and total compensation were important, but job enjoyment was equally so. My happiest years were at Morrell when I worked with a lot of great people and was a key member of a team that made the company grow into a highly respected name in the meat industry. That was the thing that was missing in my consulting work. It's a lonely type of environment and not the same kind of lasting enjoyment that comes with a job well done. The Woodhead situation was much like Morrell—great people to work with and business opportunities all over the place.

From my perspective as an outside director and chairman of the Audit Committee, I was very knowledgeable about the company's financial structure, and while the company was relatively small, it had all of the interesting accounting and financial challenges as a company ten times its size. Its opportunities for continued growth seemed unlimited. Moreover, there was absolutely no acquisition or merger talent and experience in the company, and it had all the tools needed to be very successful in the world of acquisitions and deal making—strong cash position, no long-term debt, a price earnings stock multiple of sixteen and a fabulous growth record. The company had gone public in the late sixties with annual sales a shade over $5 million and annual net income at $450,000. Ten years later, after a compounded annual growth of over twenty percent, annual sales were $37 million and net income was $3.2 million. During this period Woodhead enhanced its reputation as one of the leading producers of top quality industrial electrical products. In the financial markets its stock was rated as a jewel— having increased 700% in share value since going public in the late sixties. With these financial tools, coupled with my expertise and knowledge of the company, I was totally confident that I could quickly grow Woodhead into a much larger and even better company. After taking everything into account, I decided to join Woodhead and had a handshake agreement with the chairman of the board, a close friend for twenty years. This would be my last hurrah; we would end the marriage when I hit the magic "65"mark. I never began anything with greater expectations.

The Game Plan

Having been a director and chairman of the Audit Committee for four years coupled with my many experiences with small companies during my consulting years, I had a head start on what to expect, and what my plans would be when I took over as the CFO of the company. The first thing I did was to make my own mini due-diligence review, and it confirmed much of what I had anticipated. Many phases of the normal financial areas were in good shape thanks to a dedicated, hard working treasurer. These were insurance, cash management, and bank credit lines. Procedures for general accounting and the preparation of all subsidiary and consolidated statements were also first-rate. The statement preparation and all general ledger account details were part of a computer program developed for the company by the outside auditors, Arthur Andersen, for the mainframe computer in the corporate office. However, a number of financial areas had not been addressed, and others were in a condition requiring study and/or change. The following items in particular became major objectives in my overall game plan during my term as CFO for the company.

LIFO

The company had the perfect ingredients for adopting the LIFO inventory valuation method, but had not done the necessary leg work to make the change from FIFO.

Pension and Profit Sharing Funds

The investment performance of the fund manager had lagged terribly behind the S&P 500. The company had done little follow-up on this matter.

Bonus Plan

The company's bonus plan formula was strongly biased for certain divisions, resulting in much employee dissatisfaction. A new plan design was a must.

Tax Returns and Tax Planning

All income tax returns had been prepared by the company's outside auditors. This was costly and not efficient and should be done by the company personnel.

Preparation of the Annual Plan

This document was essentially an exercise in arithmetic prepared in large measure by the company's various controllers. No strategic planning methodologies were considered or used in the annual plan data.

Internal Auditors

The company did not have an internal auditor on the staff, but had grown to a point where it would be very cost-effective to hire one.

Organizational Responsibility

The company's organization chart clearly showed that the subsidiary president reported only to the CEO and all subsidiary employees reported only to the subsidiary president. Therefore the subsidiary controller, data processing manager, cost accounting manager, and credit manager all reported directly to the subsidiary president; corporate personnel could only offer advice. I considered this autonomous arrangement awkward, impractical, and intolerable.

Four Wall Inventory Systems

The company did not use a conventional inventory accounting method, i.e., a separate account for raw materials, work in process, and finished goods, because factory reporting data and general accounting data were not on the same wave length, and a conventional system could not be used until they were. All transactions affecting inventory were recorded in a single inventory account and necessarily required a lot of estimates (cost of sales for example). Over a year's time many mistakes were found to occur leading to large year-end physical inventory adjustments, both writedowns and write-ups. This was the Achilles heel of the accounting system.

Product Line Profitability

This company's overall gross margin of forty-five percent was phenomenal, and accordingly had not considered measuring profit by individual products. However, this financial analysis is a must in any well-run organization.

With a limited staff of only three (the treasurer/controller and two corporate accountants) it was obvious that I would have plenty of work and many interesting things to do. Besides the normal routines of a CFO, I was looking forward to organizing a program of acquisitions that could accelerate the company's growth at an even faster pace.

I've included the above detailed laundry list of things to be done because it is typical for a growth company to outpace its system of financial and management controls. When you are called upon to perform a due-diligence review on a relatively small growth company, you will probably find a number of these same items on your list of things to do.

The Box Score Part I—The Financial Department

Ten years rolled by in a hurry, and here is a report on my game plan. The bonus plan, LIFO inventory, and tax return matters were high priority items and were taken care of quickly. Shortly thereafter, the pension and profit sharing funds were transferred to a different trustee. However, it took almost eight years to completely change the preparation of the annual plan using a modern day strategic planning method. There was still a lot of satisfaction for me and my department for achieving these objectives because they were all very successful. However, it was disappointing that a board freeze on spending delayed the hiring of an internal auditor and the much needed change in the inventory system. Shortly before I retired, the board had finally approved the hiring of an internal auditor and the engagement of Arthur Andersen Consulting to install a modern system of inventory and production control. This was also a necessary ingredient for establishing a system of product line profitability. Two years before my retirement, a new CEO took over the reins and promptly revised the reporting responsibility of subsidiaries to the corporate office. It was changed to a conventional dotted line arrangement, i.e., subsidiary controllers reported to the corporate controller on all accounting matters. All of these changes were significant improvements in the company's financial system. In this respect it was far better than I had found it ten years earlier.

Box Score Part II—Company Financial Performance

Woodhead's fabulous twenty percent growth rate came to an abrupt halt in 1980. Thereafter until my retirement in 1988, the company's 1987 annual sales of $70 million only kept pace with inflation, but annual net income of $3.2 million did not keep pace. (In terms of 1979 dollars it was $2.4 million.)

Using the famed newscaster Paul Harvey's lead in: "Here's the rest of the story." In looking back at the decline of this company, I would like to share with you some observations that may be helpful as you advance in business and become a key player in a company. When I joined Daniel Woodhead Inc. as an outside director in 1975, it was truly a remarkable marketing company. Its focus was on developing specialty industrial electrical products with market niches, and marketing them through the best electrical distributors in the country. Little emphasis was placed on manufacturing because the company purchased nearly all finished parts and merely had to assemble them. Daniel Woodhead and James Edmonds were the two "architects" that made the company grow. They were chairmen of the board and CEO, respectively. Soon after I came on board, Daniel Woodhead died. A short time later, James Edmonds's health started to fail, and the CEO post was filled by a veteran company employee who had spent his long career in the production side of the business. Then, the sales manager of the company's largest subsidiary resigned because of a personal investment opportunity, and the general manager of the company's second largest subsidiary resigned to take early retirement. Unfortunately, their replacements were only mediocre performers. These personnel changes shifted the company's culture from a marketing driven company with focus on new products, new market, and gross margin to a production-minded company with emphasis on cost and expense control and investments in operations. A perfect example of this happened shortly after I became CFO. The company committed to acquire a manufacturing plant in Wales because the Welsh Government was offering numerous financial grants to U.S. companies starting up a manufacturing operation. I had to go to Wales and arrange for financing, and also to set up office and other procedures for the new plant. The financial incentives were very attractive. The problem, however, was that the company did not have the sales or marketing skills to support optimum factory production levels, and the Welsh operation lost money for seven consecutive years before making a tiny profit.

The shift in the corporation from a marketing to an operations focus and the unfortunate personnel changes had a chilling effect on growth and earnings, and it happened rather quickly. The loss of our marketing momentum produced a domino effect—sales margins declined which caused net income to decline, which caused a cry for expense reductions, which caused sharper cutbacks in new market development, new product development, and other important marketing programs such as advertising and market research. The impact of these changes caused real sales growth to come to a virtual halt. With only a fifteen percent annual growth rate yielding a fabulous gross margin of forty-five percent, the company could have reached a sales level of $150 million and a net income level of $15 million in ten years without a single acquisition of any kind. Instead, the depressed flat earnings caused a sharp decline in the market value of the stock, and therefore, ruled out the feasibility of using stock for acquisitions. During the four years I served as an outside period director, the board only considered one acquisition. The reason being that the company's thin corporate management had their hands full just keeping up with the day-to-day demands of a company growing at a twenty percent rate. The company that we did consider was a small company in Ohio that produced electrical blankets for industrial use. I personally didn't care too much about the deal because top management was "one man," the product line and the distribution didn't seem compatible, and I felt that their growth was limited. Because the purchase price was small, there was no goodwill, and the CEO was very enthusiastic about it, the board approved the deal. I remember voting a soft yes but recommended that the company consider bigger and better acquisitions in the future. Shortly after the transaction, the "one man" top management suffered a crippling heart attack, and Woodhead's top corporate management had to step in. The operations and problems of that subsidiary were a constant drain on corporate management's time; the products and distribution never did blend with the parent company's core business and the operating profits were meager at best. Seven years later I presided at the divestiture of this subsidiary, and when all the product lawsuits were finally settled, the financial box score from beginning to end was a red figure.

The bad experience with the Ohio subsidiary was more positive proof that the company's corporate staff needed help and experience, and I was excited and optimistic about the opportunity to make significant contributions to the corporate growth by acquisitions. It was therefore a great disappointment to me that I was not able to do this. Shortly after taking over as CFO, the company's growth came to an end causing a decline in the market price of the stock. A change in dividend policy caused an adverse cash flow. The tools, stock , and cash necessary to make important deals were no longer available. In my job as CFO, I assisted the operating groups who made occasional purchases of product lines, engineering drawings, etc., which were small divestitures by other companies. The operating groups also initiated the purchase of several relatively small subsidiaries. Under the company's organizational chart at the time I had to act as an advisor and helper since I did not initiate these transactions. As an advisor I warned the group of some downside risks, but they proceeded anyway. I was right, and these so called bargain purchases impacted the corporation's bottom line. The learning experience from this should be apparent. In drawing up an organizational chart, extreme care must be given not only to who reports to whom but what are the specific responsibilities of every "who."

I think all companies run into periods of difficulty, and Woodhead was no exception. Except for one year, annual net income languished at around $3 million throughout the eighties. Flat sales and lower margins accounted for much of this subpar performance, but the bottom line was also exacerbated by losses from acquisitions and substantial costs to settle product lawsuits as well as a costly protracted three-year proxy fight with Nortek, Inc., a large C-rated NYSE company.

Could the causes of all of these adversities have been avoided or minimized? Yes! Quite clearly all of the matters cited in this section required board approval and/or involvement, and therefore the directors were solely responsible for Woodhead's financial decline from superior to mediocre. During my fourteen years on the board it was always controlled by various outside directors who had numerical advantages. Every outside director was the best in his own business specialty. But as in sports where a group of all-stars doesn't necessarily make the best team, the Woodhead board never really "teamed" well. One reason might have been the fact that the board never met frequently enough for the members to truly know each other. Regularly scheduled meetings were held only four times a year. Each meeting started at 9:30 and typically ended just before lunch. There just wasn't enough time to cover all the meeting agenda items thoroughly and then get into the nuts and bolts of the business, acquisitions, and dividend policy, as well as providing the needed direction and strategic planning for management. The dividend policy is a good example. The annual cash dividend was 40¢ per share in 1979 when the earnings per share were $1.07. But in the face of declining earnings, the board raised the dividend twice during the next year—first to an annual rate of 50¢, then to an annual rate of 60¢ per share. With per share earnings of only 78¢, 91¢, 70¢, and 83¢ in the four years following the dividend increase, you can see that the impact on cash flow and working capital was serious. It resulted in the company having to borrow long-term funds to run the business, and it absolutely eliminated the possibility of making a significant acquisition for cash. How could this happen? Simple. One veteran director proposed it and the other outside directors went along with it. I was on the executive committee and had proposed no increase. I relate this to illustrate that inside directors are really lame ducks and have little or no clout in the board room.

From my own perspective, it was frustrating at times to be a bystander and see the outside directors in full control. I had to use some discretion, but I was never a wimp who rubber stamped every resolution.

These sparse comments are included as an example of the responsibility and importance of the corporate board. See Part II., Chapter 14 for more detailed comments on this subject.

I left the board a few months before my retirement as CFO of the company. Despite business differences from time to time, my last Board meeting was very cordial as usual. I told the board that I had enjoyed the association with the company very much for the past fourteen years, but also expressed disappointment in the company's lack luster financial performance over the past ten years. I gave them a number of suggestions and ideas that would get the company off the treadmill and start moving again. I reminded them that the intrinsic value of the company's name, goodwill, product line, and distribution network added up to a priceless asset that still had fantastic opportunities for growth.

My retirement date followed in a short time. It was really a fun luncheon affair. Despite the company's so-so performance, the mood and camaraderie of my staff and fellow corporate officers was always very pleasant. I had truly enjoyed my day-to-day work during my tenure as CFO. I received the usual plaque from the board for meritorious service, but also an exquisite piece of Lalique crystal that my wife absolutely treasures.

When I drove from the company parking lot that afternoon, it capped the end of a forty-year career in the financial world. I had no regrets. Overall it was a satisfying career with mostly ups, but of course a few downs. On a scale of one to ten, I would rate the experience an eight, but then I wonder if anyone ever rates their career experiences a ten.

As I drove home, I could not help but reflect on how lucky I was—a wonderful wife, son, and daughter, good health, and financial security. Tomorrow my son and I would be packing our bags for a three-week trip to the U.K. for golf in Scotland and Ireland. What a way to start retirement! Could it get any better?

****

Note: Woodhead sales started to show marked improvement in 1992, and in 1995 established an all-time record of $120 million with net income of $9.2 million. As a supportive stockholder, with many friends still working at the company, it's great news to see my old alma mater finally returning to its former growth pattern, and the stock once again enjoying a price earnings multiple in excess of sixteen times per share.

Finale

When I took that first step on LaSalle Street in the heart of Chicago's financial district some forty plus years ago, I walked into an accounting world that by today's standards was the equivalent of the Dark Ages and the horse and buggy days. Only a few offices had electric adding machines and calculators; comptometers were popular, but you needed training to acquire the skill to use them effectively; the result was that much of the tedious calculations, and simple arithmetic involving routine office work, and year-end audits were done manually. The annual closing of a company's accounting records was a laborious task, with most calendar companies struggling as late as mid-March to get the records in shape for the auditors. The big data processing companies—IBM, Burroughs, and NCR—were producing small computers, but they were essentially for billing and accounts receivable. Nevertheless, they were considered the marvel of the age and found primarily in the biggest and most profitable companies. Jobs with the Big Six firms were scarce, and the starting salary for top graduating accounting majors was $200 per month— good accounting jobs with major corporations weren't much better. The professional accountant was still perceived by much of society as "somebody good with figures." The financial statements were relatively simple and the typical report included only a few notes to the statements. The accounting impact of global business and international accounting issues were matters for only a few of America's largest international corporations. And yes, there were still offices in Chicago's famed loop using roll-top desks manned by bookkeepers wearing green eye shades and pince-nez eyeglasses.

The accounting world that you walk into will be light years ahead of the relatively primitive environment of the late forties, thanks to the amazing developments in computer hardware and software and countless high-tech inventions and innovations like the transistor, microchip, lasers, office copying and fax machines, and telecommunications. Salaries and related perks will be much improved, reflecting society's acceptance of the accountant on an equal level with other professionals.

Your work will be free of long hours of boring and rote verifications, which will be done via customized software programs. But you will face much greater intellectual challenges—some growing out of accounting and financial controls required for global business transactions as well as complex disclosures and procedures resulting from FASB, the SEC, the NYSE, and Federal Income Tax regulations. But of greater importance, you will be challenged more by CEOs who expect you to see through the labyrinths of numbers and provide their true meaning for the effective management of current operations and strategic plans for the future.

Futurists tell us that the combination of scientific discoveries, inventions and the computer development that enabled us to land our astronauts on the moon are only the tips of the iceberg as to what lies ahead. Even greater numbers of inventions and discoveries will emerge from the research centers of corporate America and our universities and colleges. Now augment this with the wealth of new knowledge from doctorate studies that are being awarded at an incredible rate of almost 3,500 per year in the United States alone. Who can calculate the impact all of this will have on business? Surely new ones will emerge, some will go out of existence, and for certain, all businesses will be affected. This world is on a course of an inexorable pursuit of change in the financial world, and it is also experiencing extensive economic and political restructuring. For the professional accountant all of these changes will bring about both opportunities and challenges to keep pace by developing new systems of controls and procedures that will effectively monitor these new enterprises.

As your business career takes form and direction, remember that good work habits and job performance, continuing self-development, integrity, and loyalty are a proven formula for getting to the top and staying there. Also remember that one of your toughest problems is time management—finding the perfect blend of time at work, time with family, and time for yourself. I have stressed this earlier in the book, and I think it is worth repeating here.

Throughout this book there are frequent passages that reflect my addiction to the game of golf. But that's understandable; I met my wonderful wife through golf, and in many other ways, golf has been extremely helpful to me in business, in my social life, and physically. It's not surprising then that I close this book with a tribute to Walter Hagan, one of golf's immortals. The "Haig" was born in 1892 and died in 1969. He won eleven major championships (second only to Jack Nicklaus's record of twenty) and was the only player to soundly beat Bobby Jones when Jones was at the peak of his game. But Hagan is remembered more because of his swashbuckling lifestyle. He was a handsome athlete who dressed like a fashion plate and from time to time, he would arrive at the golf tournaments in a limousine dressed in his tuxedo from the night before. He was the first golf professional to play with presidents, royalty, and top celebrities, and the one who elevated the image of the golf shop club-maker to a respected professional. When he finally retired and put his clubs away, he had a message for ambitious, hardworking young golf professionals. I think it's also good advice for ambitious, hard working, young accounting professionals.

Never worry. Along the way, take time to smell the flowers.

The best to all my readers...